# The Office
# (for ACCOUNTING TECHNICIANS)
# (2nd Edition)

Association of Accounting Technicians

## LEVEL 2 CERTIFICATE

**Suitable for AAT Level 2 Certificate
Working Effectively in Accounting and Finance**

# Study Manual

**Course writer
Alan Dawson, B.Ed(Hons), MAAT**

**Editor
Rose Crockett BA (Hons)**

**Published by**

**Premier**Books

Published by:

Premier Books Ltd
Prince Henry Drive
Queens Road
Immingham
North East Lincolnshire
DN40 1QY

Telephone 01469 572090

Email: info@premiertraining.co.uk
Website: www.premiertraining.co.uk

# Contents

Alan Dawson, Author

# Alan Dawson

Certificate of Education

Bachelor of Education (Hons)

Member of the Association of Accounting Technicians

Qualified NVQ Internal Verifier

Qualified NVQ Assessor

Alan is a qualified teacher. He gained his honours degree in education from Nottingham University and he went on to teach Mathematics, Modern Languages and Music in schools for 18 years.

He then turned his attention to accountancy, qualifying from the AAT and taking up various accounting roles both in private practice and industry. He spent 6 years in a large company in management accounts while at the same time taking private clients for help with bookkeeping, payroll, VAT and taxation.

From March 2006 he has been a tutor at Premier Training, with over 300 students worldwide under his guidance at one time or another.

# The Editor

## Rose Crockett

Bachelor of Arts (Hons)

Rose is a founder member of Premier Books and is a managing partner of Premier Training.

# Introduction

## A Guide to Being an Effective Accounting Technician

his study manual will provide you with all the skill to succeed in the workplace as an effective accounting technician, It will also provide all the knowledge and understanding in the Working Effectively in Accounting and Finance unit of the AAT Level 2 Certificate in Accounting. It is suitable both for home study courses and also classroom based students. All the answers to the questions have been included at the back of the book.

Being effective and efficient in dealing with financial transactions can make the difference between success and failure of any business. Keeping up-to-date with recording these transactions is just as important. A business will gain a good reputation if it pays its debts on time. It is equally important that a record of these payments is made so that others can see what has been paid and when.

All businesses have financial transactions of some sort, and all businesses must record these transactions. This book will tell you how best to deal with making and recording these transactions to ensure an efficient and effective business with a good reputation with its customers, employees and other interested parties.

# Chapter 1

## Accounting and Finance in the Workplace

In this chapter we will be looking at the differing roles within an accounting environment. We will be looking at the main functions of an accounting department in a business. We will look at the organisations themselves and how they may be structured.

In order to be effective in accounting and finance at work we need to have a basic understanding of the different roles within an accounting system as well as the different types of business.

### Bookkeeping

A bookkeeper is someone who records all the financial transactions of a business. Each type of transaction is stored in a different file called a book, hence the name bookkeeper. The most important actions of any business is buying and selling. The bookkeeper will record the details of all day to day sales and purchases in **day books**. They are called day books because daily transactions are recorded here. There will be a day book for sales and another for purchases. Obviously sales and purchases will involve the transfer of money, so the bookkeeper will also record the movement in and out of the business in a **cash book**. All books which record these transactions as they happen are called **books of prime entry**. In this case 'prime' means 'first' so these books are where the transactions are first recorded.

The bookkeeper is unlikely to be present at every transaction, so he or she will record transactions in the books of prime entry from **prime documents**. Typically a prime document is a receipt or an invoice, although other documents may fall into this category.

### Accounting

An accountant is someone who deals with the presentation and interpretation of the figures. You will see later that there are rules and regulations covering the presentation of financial information. Financial information may include a **profit & loss statement** (also known as an **income statement** or a **statement of revenue and expense**). A profit & loss statement (or P&L) shows a business's financial performance.

Financial information may also be shown in a **balance sheet** (also known as a **statement of financial position**). A balance sheet shows a business's assets, liabilities and net worth at a specific point in time.

## Accounting and Finance in the Workplace

The accountant may be responsible for advising on, and calculating taxation. Individuals and companies are all liable to taxation. Unlike employees, people with businesses are responsible for their own tax issues and the payment of amounts due. Accountants may calculate how much tax is due and complete the forms which are to be presented to **Her Majesty's Revenue and Customs** (HMRC). HMRC is the government department which deals with taxation in the UK.

When times are good, accountants are required to calculate profits. When times are bad, accountants are required to advise on how to manage risks and cut losses. Accounting can therefore be divided into two branches: financial accounting and management accounting.

The financial accountant will calculate the amount for sales revenue (also known as turnover), purchases, as well as other income and expenses so that the net profit for the year can be calculated. He/She will also record the organisation's assets and liabilities to prepare the Statement of Financial Position. In general, they are responsible for reporting the performance of the organisation as well as its financial position to the stakeholders. Stakeholders are the people who have an interest in the organisation and are directly affected by its decisions and performance, such as shareholders, banks, suppliers etc. They rely on the financial information provided by the financial accountant to make decisions. Hence, this particular branch of accounting is known as financial accounting.

Management accountants help the organisation achieve its objectives through the information they provide because it assists management in planning, controlling and making decisions. Firstly, management information is used to set standards of performance or yardsticks. For example, factory managers work with sales managers to budget production volumes to meet forecasted demands. Hence, managerial accountants can use them to analyse actual results and explain variances that occur from the budgeted results so that managers can make decisions to tackle those variances. In general, management accounting involves setting budgets/targets and analysing actual results to determine appropriate reasons for any variances.

**Finance**

Finance is essentially the opposite side of the same coin. Finance involves managing an organisation's funds to ensure that they are being used properly to achieve its objectives. Through financial analysis, companies and businesses can take decisions and monitor the sources of income and the expenses and investments that need to be made in order to stay competitive. Finance deals with the managing of funds. It involves deciding how much to invest and where to invest. It involves getting maximum returns from investments.

# CHAPTER 1
## Accounting and Finance in the Workplace

### The difference between accounting and finance

As you can see, there is a difference between the formal roles and responsibilities of an accountant and financier. However, there is a relationship between them as they cannot exist without one another and are the backbone of the organisation.

Accounting is associated with the treatment of funds and finance is associated with decision making. In accounting, the system of determining income and expenditure is based on the accrual system. Revenue is acknowledged at the point of sale and not when it was collected. Expenses are acknowledged when they are incurred rather than when they are paid. However, in finance, the system of determination of funds is based on cash flows. The revenues are acknowledged by the actual receipt in cash (cash inflow) and the expenses are acknowledged when the actual payment is made (cash outflow).

Another difference between accounting and finance is with respect to their purposes. With accounting, it aims to collect and present financial information; finance is concerned with financial strategy, managing and controlling, and decision making.

### Accounting Technician

An Accounting Technician is someone who performs some of the duties of both the bookkeeper and the accountant. He or she may assist with the preparation of financial statements, deal with bookkeeping, look after and control budgets, monitor expenses and write reports. In many larger organisations, accounting technicians work alongside members of chartered accountancy bodies. In smaller organisations, they may be the only financially trained member of staff.

In practice the roles of the bookkeeper, accountant and accounting technician are all not as clearly defined as above, but this is a guide to the traditional duties of each.

### The functions of accounting

The functions of accounting are as follows:

- **Recording**

This is the basic function of accounting. It is essentially concerned with not only ensuring that all financial business transactions are in fact recorded, but also that they are recorded in an orderly manner.

- **Classifying**

One of the basic functions of accounts in business involves properly classifying the business transactions. Financial transactions are grouped according to the needs of the company and to comply with legal and other regulations. The groups may include sales, purchases and expenses. These may be further divided into types of sale or expense. The monetary value of these divisions is grouped together into what is known as **an account.** These accounts are then grouped according to how they affect the company. Classifying accounts properly allows for quick summarisation and analysis of information.

- **Summarising**

This involves presenting the classified data in a manner which is understandable and useful to the internal as well as external users of accounting statements. This process leads to the preparation of the Income Statement and Balance Sheet.

- **Analysis and Interpretation**

The recorded financial data is analysed and interpreted in a manner that the end-users can make a meaningful judgment about the financial condition and profitability of the business.

- **Forecasting**

The data is also used for preparing the future plan and framing of policies for executing such plans.

- **Communicating**

The accounting information, after being meaningfully analysed and interpreted, has to be communicated in a proper form and manner to the proper person. This is done through preparation and distribution of accounting reports, which include, besides the usual income statement and the balance sheet, additional information in the form of accounting ratios, graphs, diagrams, cash flow statements etc.

- **Internal Auditing**

Internal auditors, although employed by or contracted to a business, are not responsible for carrying out company activities. Internal auditors advise management regarding how to better execute their responsibilities. Internal auditing involves checking that the company's policies and procedures are being followed.

- **External Auditing**

An external auditor is a person or group of people who check that the financial transactions have been recorded accurately and in accordance with legal requirements. The external auditor is independent of the entity being audited. Users of these entities' financial information, such as shareholders, investors, government agencies, and the general public, rely on the external auditor to present an unbiased and **independent** audit report.

## Types of Business

There are two main sectors of business; the private sector and the public sector. The private sector consists of businesses that are owned by private individuals or groups of individuals. The public sector consists of entities overseen or owned by either central government or local government.

## Sole Trader

The business will be owned and run by an individual. He or she will probably be responsible for most of the running of the business. He or she will be in charge of buying and selling goods or services and be in charge of hiring and firing staff. Many sole traders maintain their own books and then employ an accountant to prepare the final accounts ready for the tax calculation at the end of each financial year.

It is important to remember that a sole trader not only has the rights to all the profits a business makes, but also he or she is personally responsible for any losses. If a sole trader finds that he or she cannot pay his or her creditors from the business's income, then the money has to be found from the sole trader's personal belongings. For example, if a sole trader cannot keep up the repayments on the loan secured from the bank, the bank has the right to any or all of the sole trader's personal belongings until the debt has been repaid or the sole trader has no more belongings.

## Partnerships

This is where a group of individuals come together to form a business. Typically there will be two to twenty individuals in a partnership and an agreement will have been made as to the proportion of profits to which each partner will be entitled. Partnerships are formed usually because, with more people involved in the business, there will be more expertise and money available to invest the company.

However, as with sole traders, the partners are personally responsible for any losses. In England and Wales they are 'jointly' responsible. All partners are equally responsible for all the debts of the business. They can only be sued as a group and not as an individual. In Scotland the law is slightly different. Here they are 'jointly and severally' liable, which means that in certain cases an individual partner can be sued, but if this partner doesn't have the resources to cover the suit then the other partners become liable for any amounts due.

Many partnerships are now becoming Limited Liability Partnerships (LLP). This is where the partners are only liable for amounts up to their investment in the company. Unlike sole traders or ordinary partnerships, a partner is responsible for losses only up to the amount which that partner has as equity in the business.

**Limited Company**

A limited company is where a business is formed which is quite separate in legal terms from its 'owners'. The owners are **shareholders** but the company's finances are separate from the shareholders' personal finances. The shareholders have 'limited liability', meaning that they are only responsible for the amount of money they have invested (or guaranteed) to the company.

There are two main types of limited company. A **private limited company** may have one or more shareholders. The shares cannot be offered to the public. A **public limited company** (plc) must have at least two shareholders and must have issued shares worth at least £50,000. Both kinds of limited company must be registered at **Companies House** and each must appoint a director (at least two if it's a plc) who will manage the business. Each year a limited company must file its accounts with Companies House where the figures are open to the public. Profits are distributed to the shareholders each year (called **dividends**) in proportion to the number of shares owned. Some of the profit may be retained by the company for use within the company to pay future debts or for future investments.

**Public Sector**

Public sector businesses are owned or controlled by the Government and ultimately paid for by the tax payer. The public sector covers a wide range of organisations with different functions e.g.
- Central government
- Local government
- Health trusts
- Educational bodies e.g. schools and colleges

There are independent public sector organisations such as the BBC. The BBC is under the control of a board of governors appointed by the Queen but nominated by the Prime Minister. Funding for the BBC comes largely from the TV licence payer.

Public sector organisations do not set out to make a profit, but any losses are covered by the tax payer.

**Other Business Types**

**Co-operatives**

Co-operatives are owned by their staff who are 'members' of the company. Profits are shared amongst the members. Losses too are shared.

**Franchises**

A franchise business is a business in which the owners, or franchisors, sell the rights to their business logo and model to third parties. The third party is called a franchisee. The franchisee is essentially buying the right to use a business brand, but must adhere to certain restrictions imposed by the franchisor. For example, the franchisee may be compelled to buy equipment and supplies from the franchisor, or those recommended by the franchisor. Uniforms and signs may also be determined by the franchisor.

Well known brands which are franchises include McDonalds, Hilton Hotels, United Carpets and Subway.

**Not for Profit Businesses**

This includes charities or clubs. Typically they will have been established with the objective of addressing a social need, rather than simply to provide a service or generate revenue. They receive funds from individuals or groups. They will reinvest revenue for the purpose of serving their client group or achieving their objective.

**Organisational Structures**

It may be becoming clear that the organisational structure of a business is dependent on the type of business. A small sole trader may do all the bookkeeping him- or herself. This is perfectly possible (although a lot of hard work) since the amount of information required will be limited. Basically all that is required in a one-man business is a list of what was sold and a list of what was bought. Taking the books to an accountant each year will be sufficient for the sole trader to see how well (or otherwise) the business is going and to satisfy HMRC regarding taxation.

In partnerships a little more work is required, although each partner will be responsible for his or her own tax liabilities. Since the company has more than one owner, a track of sales and purchases needs to be kept and the revenue and expenses created by each partner. It would be wise for a partnership to employ at least a bookkeeper to record the day to day transactions.

Limited companies will require more detailed accounting records. The format of the accounting records is regulated and more than simply what was bought and sold will need to be recorded and reported. Larger companies will have different departments for sales, purchases, wages, and **management accounts**. Management accountants assist management in decision-making, planning, and control. **Financial accountants** report the financial position and performance of a business.

Where there is more than one person in a company some sort of organisational structure will be required. Employees must be aware of their reporting structure. It is vital for the efficient running of a business that each individual knows who will be providing information and also who this information should be passed on to.

The most common structure for larger businesses is the **hierarchical structure**. Responsibility passes from the director, to senior management, to middle management, and then to supervisors.

Then there is the 'tall' structure. This has many levels of management with a long chain of responsibility.

Another structure is the 'flat' structure.

The following pages show each structure in diagrammatic form.

## Hierarchical Structure

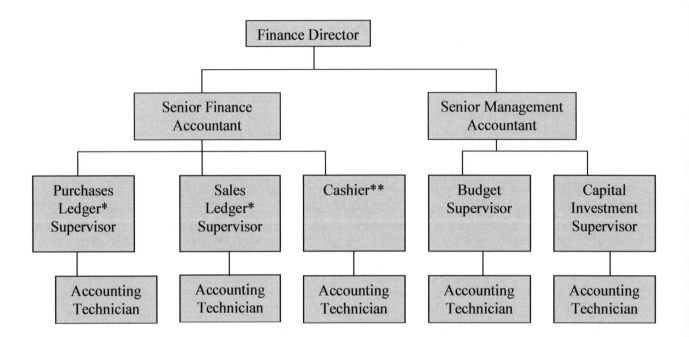

*A purchase ledger is the book (now more commonly stored on a computer) where all transactions with suppliers to whom the business owes money is recorded. Similarly a sales ledger is the book where all transactions with customers who owe money to the business is recorded. More details of these are given in the book Basic Accounting I & II by the same author.

**A Cashier is a person who deals with all the cash transactions of a business. Again, more details can be found in Basic Accounting I & II by the same author.

## Tall Structure

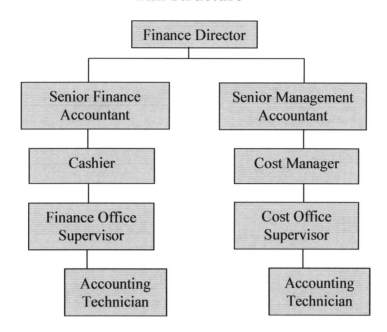

## Flat Structure

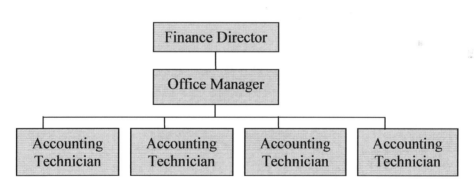

Each of the above structures has been shown in a **functional format**, with each position showing what its function is. They could have been shown by **regional area** (Finance Director North and Finance Director South for example), by **product** (Finance Director Private Vehicles and Finance Director Commercial Vehicles), or a structure could be set up for individual projects.

# CHAPTER 1
## Accounting and Finance in the Workplace

**Reporting Lines**

No matter what the business or how it is structured all businesses carry out transactions which are common to all.

- All businesses sell goods or services
- All businesses purchase goods and services and pay expenses
- All businesses pay money into a bank account and make payments from it
- All businesses pay wages or a remuneration of some kind.

All these transactions must be recorded in some form. Some small businesses simply collect all **invoices** and **receipts** and give them to the accountant at the end of the year so that the accountant can produce financial statements from them. An invoice is a list of goods or services sold and given to the purchaser for payment. A receipt is a written acknowledgement that payment has been made for goods or services. Some small businesses record these transactions in their books as they occur, making the accountant's work easier and less time consuming (and therefore usually less expensive). A larger business will need to employ staff to look after the recording of these transactions since it will not be physically possible to do this on one's own. The record of the transactions can be kept either by hand (manually) or on a computer, but at some stage this information will need to be passed on to other members of the business.

Whatever the structure of the business you must be aware of the reporting lines. The accounting technician must know, for example, whether to report to the office manager or the payroll supervisor. Most companies supply an organisational chart similar to those shown on the previous page. They may include the actual names of the people so they may need to be updated periodically.

What information you will need to report and in what format will be determined by person to whom it is to be reported. We will look at how to report information later in this book.

There may be specific tasks which do not follow the normal reporting lines. The cashier's assistant may need information from the payroll assistant for the weekly cash wages. The stores manager may require certain information from the accounting technician without going through the office manager.

It is critical that all employees should know the identity and status of the person to whom they should report and also what information is required and the format in which it should be presented.

Accounting tasks should be checked, usually by a more senior person. Invoices, for example, should be checked for accuracy. Accounting tasks should be authorised. Payment of invoices, for example, should be authorised by a senior person.

If the correct reporting lines are not followed, losses could be made and the reputation of the company could be damaged. If the wrong person is given the information, time will be lost and ultimately purchases, sales, receipts and payments could be missed or delayed.

Communicating the correct information in the correct format to the correct person is vital if the business is to perform efficiently and effectively.

## Chapter Summary

- A bookkeeper records the financial transactions of a business in day books, while an accountant presents and interprets this data. A financier manages the assets of a company and advises on how best to invest the assets.

- The functions of an accountant are: recording, classifying, summarising, analysing, interpreting and communicating financial data. The accountant may also check the accuracy of the records.

- Organisations fall broadly into two main categories; public sector and private sector.

- There are three main types of private sector organisation: sole traders, partnerships and limited companies.

- Public sector organisations are owned by the government (or local government) and are paid for to a large extent by the tax payer.

- All businesses need an organisational structure of some kind.

- For the effective and efficient running of a business, all employees should be aware of the organisational structure and the correct reporting lines within that structure.

# Practice Questions

## Chapter 1

**1.1**

i)      Traditionally, if you record day to day transactions in books of prime entry would your job be in:

      a)     Bookkeeping
      b)     Accounting
      c)     Finance

ii)     Traditionally, if you advise on the best shares in which to invest surplus funds would your job be in:

      a)     Bookkeeping
      b)     Accounting
      c)     Finance

iii)    Traditionally, if you prepare a Profit & Loss account and a Balance Sheet would your job be in:

      a)     Bookkeeping
      b)     Accounting
      c)     Finance

**1.2**

Your organisation is in the process of employing a bookkeeper in the accounts department.

Explain at least 3 of the tasks that the bookkeeper may carry out

**1.3**

i)    An auditor will:

    a)    Prepare the annual Income Statement

    b)    Set the budget for the next 3 months

    c)    Check the accuracy of the company's recorded profit.

ii)    A financial accountant will:

    a)    Prepare the annual Income Statement

    b)    Set the budget for the next 3 months

    c)    Check the accuracy of the company's recorded profit.

iii)    A management accountant will:

    a)    Prepare the annual Income Statement

    b)    Set the budget for the next 3 months

    c)    Check the accuracy of the company's recorded profit.

**1.4**

Very briefly explain the difference between accounting and finance.

**1.5**

Very briefly explain the difference between an internal auditor and an external auditor.

.

**1.6**

a)      What type of business is run and owned by an individual?

b)      What type of business is owned by its shareholders?

c)      What type of business is run and owned by a group of associated people?

d)      What type of business is run or controlled by the government?

e)      What type of business is run and owned by its staff?

f)      What type of business is licensed to a third party?

g)      If you bought shares from a stockbroker who traded in shares on the stock market, what kind of business would you be investing in?

**1.7**

i)      As an Accounting Technician, you work in an organisation with a long chain of command. There are many levels of management and supervision. Is this likely to be

      a)      A Hierarchical structure
      b)      A Tall structure
      c)      A Flat Structure?

ii)     As an Accounting Technician, you work in an organisation with few layers of management. You are responsible to the office manager, who oversees all of your colleagues as well. The office manager is responsible directly to the Managing Director. Is this likely to be

      a)      A Hierarchical structure
      b)      A Tall structure
      c)      A Flat Structure?

iii)    As an Accounting Technician, you work in an organisation where you are responsible to a manager for your area of work. Other managers are responsible for colleagues who work in other areas of accounts. There are various levels within the organisation and at each stage one person has a number of workers directly under them according to their area of work. Is this likely to be

a)      A Hierarchical structure
b)      A Tall structure
c)      A Flat Structure


**1.8**

Below is an extract from an organisational chart showing the structure of a business.

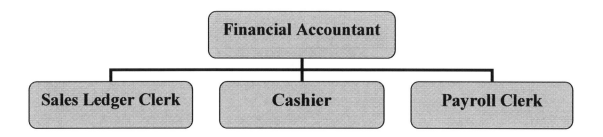

a)      Identify the three reporting lines

b)      The financial accountant has received a query from a customer about an outstanding balance. Who would the financial accountant ask?

c)      The payroll clerk pays staff who are paid weekly in cash. From whom would they need to request the correct notes and coins?

d)      The cashier always receives details for the amounts required by the payroll department for staff wages late. To whom should they complain?

e)      The business buys and sells goods on credit. What role appears to be missing from the chart?

**1.9**

Explain what the following are

a) A public sector company

b) A shareholder

c) A stakeholder

d) A not for profit business.

e) A plc.

# Chapter 2

## The Need for Efficient Accounting

In this chapter we will be looking at why accounting records are kept. We will look at solvency and the penalties if a company becomes insolvent. We will look at how keeping accounting records efficiently can guard against the risks of becoming insolvent.

Before we know how to be efficient in accounting we need to know why we are keeping financial records.

We have already seen that financial information is useful to stakeholders. Stakeholders need to know that the company with which they are dealing will be able to produce enough sales to satisfy its customers and generate enough revenue to pay its creditors.

We have also seen that financial information is useful to managers. Managers can plan for the future using the information provided by financial information.

Accounting information is also used by other departments within the organisation. The sales ledger information can be used by the sales representatives, showing those customers who place frequent orders, those that may be persuaded to place more orders, and those who are slow payers. The information provided by the cashier can be used by the buying department. Buyers will need to know whether purchases can be paid for in cash or whether credit facilities must be sought. Purchase ledger information will show the administration department how much is owed in overhead expenses and whether the overhead must be cut back or whether it can be developed.

**Efficiency in an Organisation**

For financial information to be of use it must be:

- Complete
- Accurate
- Timely

The sales representative may waste time and effort if only some of the customer accounts are available to him/her.

Managers may spend money on project they can't afford if the amount of profit generated by the business is not accurate.

Investors will seek other investments if the information presented is not up-to-date. An investor will not speculate in the business if the information is several months old.

# CHAPTER 2
## The Need for Efficient Accounting

Efficiency can be defined as acting with a minimum of waste, expense, or unnecessary effort. If the accounting information is supplied complete, accurate and on time, it will certainly contribute to the efficient running of the organisation.

### Solvency

A business must be solvent. Solvency means being able to meet financial obligations when they are due. If a company cannot pay its debts it becomes insolvent. The consequences of being insolvent can be disastrous.

An individual can become **bankrupt**. This applies to sole traders and partners in a partnership. The individual can voluntarily go bankrupt or if a creditor is owed more than £750. The creditor can apply for a compulsory bankruptcy order, provided certain formalities have been followed. Bankruptcy effectively relieves the individual from all debts, but only after the individuals assets have been handed over to a trustee. The individual's assets are not confined to the business assets, but will include their personal assets including their home. The proceeds of the sale of the individual's assets will be used to pay the creditors. Debtors are usually discharged from their debts one year after the date of the bankruptcy order. However, the individual will be forced to stop trading and the individual's credit rating will be affected for 6 years. This will result in difficulties in getting credit or even opening a bank account. Bankruptcy must be publicly advertised.

In legal terms a company does not become bankrupt (although it is commonly called this in the media). A company may at first go into **administration.** Contrary to popular belief, an administrator's function is not to close the company, but to keep it going. A company may appoint an 'administrator' itself. The courts do not have to be involved at this point. Creditors may apply to the courts for an administrator to be appointed. The administrator can make whatever changes are necessary to keep the company going or they can sell off assets in favour of the creditors if they see fit.

A company may go into **voluntary liquidation**. To liquidate means to convert to cash. If a company goes into voluntary liquidation then a creditors meeting must be called so that they can appoint a liquidator. The liquidator will then sell the company's assets and distribute the proceeds amongst the creditors. There is an order of priority of creditors, so it is possible that some creditors will get nothing at all. Unpaid tax is top of the priority order. Employees are regarded as creditors and will receive up to £800 each in redundancy and back pay. Bottom of the priority list are the unsecured creditors. These will include the company's suppliers of goods.

When everything else fails a creditor who is owed more than £750 can present a **winding up order** to the court. The company will then have one last chance to pay the outstanding amount. Once the winding up order has been agreed by the court then the banks will freeze the company's account and all trading (including share trading) must stop. If the company cannot pay the outstanding amount it will be **compulsorily liquidated.**

# CHAPTER 2
## The Need for Efficient Accounting

**Avoiding insolvency**

You may now be wondering what this has to do with efficient accounting. Well, let us suppose that you open a new business with a loan from the bank. Your first 3 months have gone really well. You have negotiated credit terms of 30 days with several suppliers and you have made sales of £20,000 even though you have been pressured into offering 60 days credit.

Now, after 3 months, you start to realise difficulties. You have to pay your suppliers after 30 days but you must wait 60 days for the cash to arrive from your customers. Matters are made worse by the fact that some customers are not paying on time. Your funds have been going down steadily in the bank and you have accrued a £3000 unauthorised overdraft at the bank. Because you have been so busy you have neglected to pay one of your large suppliers and they are threatening to stop supplying you unless the overdue amount is paid immediately. The bank also wants you to talk to them about the large (and increasing) unauthorised overdraft and one of your customers hasn't made a payment at all on any of the goods they have bought.

So, in spite of good sales, the poor management of cash is turning this into a dangerous situation. Your company could very soon become insolvent. What you need is **working capital**.

Working capital is the surplus of money in, money due in and money that can be quickly realisable over money due to be paid out. (Realisable means to bring in money by means of sale). In the example above there is little or no working capital. Efficient accounting would have brought the problems to light a lot sooner and remedies could have been put in place to ensure that solvency was maintained.

What could the accounting technician have told you? Well firstly, having customers pay much later than you pay suppliers is not a good idea. The accounting technician would tell you to negotiate longer payment terms with your suppliers or shorter payment terms with your customers or both.

You should chase up slow paying customers by efficient records of sales and payment by your customers. Your accounting technician could send you weekly records of debtors and their payments as well as forecasts of what is due and when.

Receipts from customers should be banked as soon as possible. This is important from a security point of view, but also cheques take 4 days before funds can be drawn on them. The longer you keep a cheque the later you can access the funds from it. Records of what has been received and what has been banked should be kept up-to-date.

Accurate and up-to-date records should be kept of what has been bought from suppliers and what has been paid. Your accounting technician could send you weekly records of creditors and your payments to them as well as forecasts of what is due and when.

Chase slow paying customers. You may also offer an incentive to pay early such as a discount for cash. It is also possible to charge extra for late payments but you must be mindful that you might annoy your customers with this approach.

# CHAPTER 2
## The Need for Efficient Accounting

Your accounting technician should also check the bank statement monthly. Due to timing differences the bank statement may not be accurate so you should keep your own records of cash in and cash out. (Remember that in accounting 'cash' means cheques and bank transfers as well as notes and coins). You should reconcile the bank statement to the cash book monthly so that you are aware of how much money is in the bank at any time.

A cash flow forecast should be prepared. This would show money that is due in as well as money that is due out. This will ensure that you are aware of any problems with working capital in the future.

If a temporary shortfall in working capital is expected then negotiate an authorised overdraft with the bank. Banks are usually quite happy to authorise this if supported by evidence that the overdraft will be paid back.

You can see therefore that complete, accurate and timely records of cash transactions can mean the difference between success and failure of a business.

## Chapter Summary

- Accounting records of a business are kept for the use of many different types of user.

- Financial information must be complete, accurate and timely for the efficient running of a business.

- **Solvency** means being able to meet financial obligations when they are due.

- An individual can become **bankrupt** if they become insolvent.

- A company can go into **administration** or go into **liquidation** if it becomes insolvent

- To avoid insolvency a company must have **working capital**.

- Accounting records which are efficiently kept can help to avoid a company or individual becoming insolvent.

# **Practice Questions**

## **Chapter 2**

**2.1**

Which of the following best describes efficiency?

a)      Doing everything as quickly as possible.

b)      Always following the rules and regulations as shown in the company policy.

c)      Completing tasks with a minimum of waste, expense, and unnecessary effort.

d)      Completing tasks as cheaply as possible.

**2.2**

Which of the following best describes solvency?

a)      Having plenty of money in the bank.

b)      Being able to pay debts when they are due.

c)      Not having any loans or debts.

d)      Not having any overdue credit customers.

**2.3**

Which of the following best describes working capital?

a)      The money in the bank.

b)      The money due to the company from its credit customers.

c)      The money the company can raise from cash sales.

d)      The surplus of money the company already has plus the money due in against the money due to be paid out.

# CHAPTER 2
## The Need for Efficient Accounting

**2.4**

One of your customers has an overdue invoice of £1000. The customer was allowed 30 days to pay but it is now 45 days old. What is the best course of action?

a)      Send a reminder letter.

b)      Do nothing as you don't want to upset the customer; they may go elsewhere for their goods in future.

c)      Present a winding up order to the court

d)      Employ a debt collection agency to recover the money.

Explain your why you chose your answer and why you rejected the others.


**2.5**

What 3 fundamental rules must be followed if financial information is to be useful?


**2.6**

Suggest 3 separate financial records which should be kept to help a company remain solvent.


**2.7**

If a company goes into administration, the administrator's principle function is which of the following?

a)      To close the business

b)      The find ways of keeping the business going

c)      To sell all the company's assets

d)      To prevent the company from trading


**2.8**

What is the difference between bankruptcy and liquidation?

# Chapter 3

## Company Policies and Procedures

In this chapter we will be looking at why accounting records are kept. We will look at solvency and the penalties if a company becomes insolvent. We will look at how keeping accounting records efficiently can guard against the risks of becoming insolvent.

All businesses need policies and procedures. As we have seen, there are processes within an organisation which are fundamental to the success of the business. These processes must be properly guided by management, performed in a consistent way, ensure the needs of the organisation are met and the correct information is collected and communicated to others. In addition, a company's policies and procedures will ensure that the organisation complies with legal requirements.

The procedures may be to ensure safety, confidentiality, maintaining quality, maintaining the correct image for the company, or simply guidance. Procedures do not have to be written, but those which are not written can lead to unacceptably different approaches, which can result in inconsistent and inefficient practices, and conflict between staff members.

A company will produce written procedures for as many different topics as it feels necessary, but for accountancy and finance it should include:

- A code of conduct
- Health & Safety
- Confidentiality
- Maintaining accounting records
- Ordering goods and services
- Making Payments
- Payroll processing
- Retaining documents.
- 'Green' issues

Some of the areas described above are covered by legislation. (Legislation means laws and rules made by the government).

# CHAPTER 3
## Company Policies and Procedures

**Code of Conduct**

A code of conduct is a set of rules outlining the proper practices and responsibilities for an individual within an organisation. It often consists of things to do in certain situations and sets out require standards of behaviour. What you view as proper conduct may be considered inappropriate behaviour to others.

What goes into a code of conduct will vary from company to company. Most will cover items such as not turning up for work under the influence of alcohol or drugs and not using the computers for social networking. Obviously these affect the efficiency of workplace. Some codes of conduct will set dress codes or restrict items you may have in your work area. If you work in an office where customers or suppliers can see, the company will want to give a positive image. While torn jeans and an untidy work environment may be acceptable in some situations, they will be inappropriate where the company aims to portray a professional image. You may feel this is unfair, but if the customer is not convinced of the image the company portrays they will go elsewhere.

**Health & Safety**

Employers have responsibilities for the health and safety of their employees. They are also responsible for any visitors to their premises such as customers, suppliers and the general public.

There are many different laws which cover Health & Safety but **The Health and Safety at Work Act 1974** is the primary piece of legislation covering work-related health and safety in the United Kingdom. The Act sets out the general duties which employers have towards their employees and the general public. It requires employers of five or more people to have a written statement of health and safety policy. It need not be complicated and many policy documents are no longer than one page.

A written statement should have three parts:

A general statement of intent.

This should outline in broad terms the organisation's overall philosophy in relation to the management of health and safety, including reference to the broad responsibilities of both management and workforce.

People and their duties

Who is responsible for what.

Arrangements

Details of how the statement of intent will be carried out.

# CHAPTER 3
## Company Policies and Procedures

Most statements of general policy will state:

- that the business is committed to keeping employees, customers and anyone else affected by the business' activities safe

- that there is a commitment to engaging and consult with employees on day-to-day health and safety conditions and provide advice and supervision on occupational health

- that there is an understanding of the legal duty to provide a safe working environment, safe work equipment and safe methods of work

An employer must appoint someone competent to help meet the health and safety duties. This could be the employer or it could be someone appointed by the employer (a Health & Safety Officer).

The arrangements section of the health and safety policy should say how the commitments made in the general statement of intent will be met. This part of the policy deals with the practical arrangements by which the policy will be effectively implemented. These include:

- safety training;
- safe systems of work;
- safe place of work;
- machine/area guarding;
- utilisation of safety committee(s) and safety representatives;
- fire safety and prevention;
- medical facilities and welfare;
- maintenance of records;
- accident reporting and investigation;
- emergency procedures;
- and workplace monitoring.

The policy must be signed by the employer.

The Health and Safety at Work Act also sets out the duties the employees have to themselves and each other. The most important responsibilities as an employee are:

- to take reasonable care of their own health and safety

- to take reasonable care not to put other people - fellow employees and members of the public - at risk by what they do or don't do in the course of their work

- to co-operate with the employer, making sure they get proper training and they understand and follow the company's health and safety policies

- not to interfere with or misuse anything that's been provided for their health, safety or welfare

- to report any injuries, strains or illnesses suffered as a result of doing their job

The employee should deal with any avoidable hazards, either by putting them right themselves (such as moving obstacles from fire exits or tidying trailing electricity leads) or reporting problems to the relevant person (such as insufficient light on the stairs or heavy items stored insecurly on high shelves).

The Health and Safety at Work Act qualified the duties of the employer by the clause 'so far as is reasonably practicable'. This means that the employer doesn't have to take measures to avoid the risk if the cost or trouble is greatly disproportionate to the risk. Extreme examples might be:

- To spend £1m to prevent five staff suffering bruised knees is obviously grossly disproportionate; but

- To spend £1m to prevent a major explosion capable of killing 150 people is obviously proportionate.

Failure to comply with Health & Safety law can result in fines or, in the most serious of cases, imprisonment for up to two years.

**The Management of Health and Safety at Work Regulations 1999** give details of what the employers are required to do to implement the Health and Safety at Work Act. The main requirement is that every employer must make a suitable and sufficient assessment of the risks to the health and safety of his/her employees to which they are exposed whilst they are at work, and the risks to health and safety of those not employed by the business but associated with it (such as customers). A self-employed person must assess the risks to his/her own health and safety. If the employer employs five or more employees, a written record of the findings must be recorded.

**The Health and Safety Information for Employees Regulations 1989** requires that employers display an approved poster in the workplace. Alternatively the employer may provide an approved leaflet to each employee. The approved leaflet is shown on the next two pages.

Health and Safety
Executive

# Health and Safety Law

What you need to know

This is a web-friendly
version of pocket card
ISBN 978 0 7176 6350 7,
published 04/09

All workers have a right to work in places where risks
to their health and safety are properly controlled. Health
and safety is about stopping you getting hurt at work or
ill through work. Your employer is responsible for health
and safety, but you must help.

## What employers must do for you

1   Decide what could harm you in your job and the precautions to stop it. This is
    part of risk assessment.
2   In a way you can understand, explain how risks will be controlled and tell you
    who is responsible for this.
3   Consult and work with you and your health and safety representatives in
    protecting everyone from harm in the workplace.
4   Free of charge, give you the health and safety training you need to do your job.
5   Free of charge, provide you with any equipment and protective clothing you
    need, and ensure it is properly looked after.
6   Provide toilets, washing facilities and drinking water.
7   Provide adequate first-aid facilities.
8   Report major injuries and fatalities at work to our Incident Contact Centre:
    **0845 300 9923**. Report other injuries, diseases and dangerous incidents online
    at **www.hse.gov.uk**.
9   Have insurance that covers you in case you get hurt at work or ill through work.
    Display a hard copy or electronic copy of the current insurance certificate where
    you can easily read it.
10  Work with any other employers or contractors sharing the workplace or
    providing employees (such as agency workers), so that everyone's health and
    safety is protected.

## What you must do

1   Follow the training you have received when using any work items your employer
    has given you.
2   Take reasonable care of your own and other people's health and safety.
3   Co-operate with your employer on health and safety.
4   Tell someone (your employer, supervisor, or health and safety representative) if
    you think the work or inadequate precautions are putting anyone's health and
    safety at serious risk.

**If there's a problem**

1   If you are worried about health and safety in your workplace, talk to your employer, supervisor, or health and safety representative.
2   You can also look at our website for general information about health and safety at work.
3   If, after talking with your employer, you are still worried, you can find the address of your local enforcing authority for health and safety and the Employment Medical Advisory Service via HSE's website: **www.hse.gov.uk**

**Fire safety**

You can get advice on fire safety from the Fire and Rescue Services or your workplace fire officer.

**Employment rights**

Find out more about your employment rights at:
**www.direct.gov.uk**

All firms with more than 10 employees are required to keep a record of accidents. This is a requirement of the **Social Security (Claims and Payments) Regulations 1979**. Accident books are available from the Health and Safety Executive (HSE). HSE is the national independent watchdog for work-related health, safety and illness. It is an independent regulator and acts in the public interest to reduce work-related death and serious injury in Britain's workplaces. The accident books are designed to record accidents but maintain confidentiality. They also give basic first aid advice and set out the employees duties under RIDDOR (see below).

Any employee who suffers a personal injury through an accident at work must inform his or her employer as soon as possible after the accident occurred. The employer must then take reasonable steps to investigate the circumstances of the accident.

The following information must be recorded about each incident:

- Name, address and occupation of the injured person

- Date and time of the accident

- Place where the accident happened

- Cause and nature of the injury

- Name, address and occupation of the person reporting the accident if this is not the injured person

If the accident or injury is not minor, the employer must report the incident to either the Local Authority Environmental Health Department or the local Health and Safety executive. This is another legal requirement covered in the **Reporting of Injuries, Diseases and Dangerous Occurrences Regulations 1995** (or RIDDOR).

The incidents involving staff which must be reported are:

- Death

- Major Injuries (such as fractures, dislocations, loss of sight, or injuries leading to unconsciousness)

- Accidents resulting in the employee being away from work for more than three days. From April 2012 this increased to more than seven days.

- Reportable diseases

- Dangerous occurrences (even if there were no injuries). For example, a building under construction collapsing.

- Gas incidents

A list of exactly what must be reported is published by HSE and is available at http://www.hse.gov.uk/riddor/what-must-i-report.htm

**The Regulatory Reform (Fire Safety) Order 2005** requires that a 'responsible person' (the owner or employer or a person appointed by them) must carry out a fire risk assessment.to ensure that the current fire precautions are adequate. This must be a written document if there are 5 or more employees.

The fire precautions must include:

- means of detection and giving warning in case of fire

- the provision of means of escape

- the provision of emergency lighting to escape routes

- means of fighting fire (where necessary)

- the training of staff in fire safety

- the publication of an "emergency plan" & the "fire safety procedures" for a specific building

The local Fire Authority is responsible for enforcement. They may visit premises and may make recommendations for improvements. If the improvements are not carried out within a reasonable time an Enforcement Notice can be issued by the Fire Authority. In these cases the Fire Authority is legally bound to publish the name of the 'responsible person' and the premises to which it applies.

In extreme cases the Fire Authority can issue a Prohibition Notice which prevents the building being used at all.

If the Enforcement Notice or Prohibition notice is ignored, a fine will be imposed or even a prison sentence.

**The Health and Safety (Display Screen Equipment) Regulations 1992** requires that employers must carry out a risk assessment of all workstations used by employees. A workstation is a computer and monitor, software and other hardware, the desk, chair and work surface and the immediate environment. A risk assessment will cover items such as:

- Is the screen free from flicker?

- Does the screen swivel and tilt?

- Is the screen free from glare?

- Is the keyboard at a suitable height and are all the characters on it easily readable?

- Is the mouse in a suitable position?

- Is the work surface large enough for the monitor and necessary papers and documents?

- Is there sufficient lighting?

- Is the chair adjustable for height and is the back adjustable for height and tilt?

- Is the work area warm enough and not too noisy?

HSE provide a checklist form which covers the requirements for the risk assessment.

The regulations state that employees should have regular breaks. The frequency of these breaks is not set, but suggests that a 5 or 10 minute break every hour is better than a 15 minute break every 2 hours. Breaks may occur naturally in the employee's work routine, but if not then set breaks should be introduced.

The employer must provide for an eye test when the employee requests one. This must be provided free of charge. The employer is only responsible for the cost of spectacles where they are used solely for display screen work.

The employer must also ensure that the equipment and furniture conform to certain standards. These include:

- The display screen should be of a suitable size and the characters must be clear and well-defined

- The space in front of the keyboard should be sufficient to provide support for the hands and upper arms

- There should be sufficient space around the computer for the user to find a comfortable position

- The chair must be adjustable in height and have an adjustable back rest.

- There should be sufficient lighting and there should be no glare

---

**LEARNING POINT**

For the AAT assessment, you won't need to know the precise content of the regulations, but you will need to know that these areas are covered by legal requirements. Knowledge of the individual laws is not required.

---

Health & Safety in the workplace is covered by numerous pieces of legislation. Not all the laws have been covered here. Some relate to certain business types such as mining and nuclear industries while others relate to certain types of hazards such as chemicals and asbestos. Those who are involved with Health & Safety should visit the HSE website at www.hse.gov.uk , where all Health & Safety matters are covered.

# CHAPTER 3
## Company Policies and Procedures

**Confidentiality**

Businesses have a duty to keep personal information secret. If it is not kept secret personal details may find their way into the public domain which individuals don't always want and in some cases can be detrimental to the individual involved. Business activities may find their way to competitors if information is not kept confidential.

**The Data Protection Act 1998** regulates how personal information is used and prevents misuse of personal details.

**Data** means any information which is held either on a computer or manually.
**Personal data** means data which relate to a living individual. It is not personal data if, for example, you have records of the number of customers visiting your shop, but it is personal data if those customers can be identified, even if only by a reference number.
**Data subject** means an individual who is the subject of personal data
**Data controller** means, a person or persons who determine the purposes for which and the manner in which any personal data are processed
**Data processor**, in relation to personal data, means any person (other than an employee of the data controller) who processes the data on behalf of the data controller.

The Data Protection Principles are:

**1.** Data should be processed fairly and lawfully

**2.** Data should be obtained and processed for specific purposes

**3.** Data should be adequate, relevant and not excessive in relation to the purpose or purposes for which it is processed

**4.** Data should be accurate and kept up to date

**5.** Data should not be kept for longer than is necessary

**6.** Data must be processed in accordance with the rights of the data subject

**7.** Data must be kept securely

**8.** Data should not to be transferred outside the EU or the European Economic Area unless the country in question has an adequate level of protection for data

You cannot process personal data unless it is covered by any one of the following:

- The data subject has given his consent to the processing

- The data processing is necessary for the performance of a contract

- The processing is necessary for compliance with any legal obligation

- The processing is necessary in order to protect the vital interests of the data subject

- The data processing is necessary for the administration of justice or in the public interest

- The processing is necessary for the purposes of legitimate interests pursued by the data controller

The Act gives data subjects rights to access personal data about themselves which is held in either computerised or manual form. This extends to a description of the data held, the purposes for which it is processed and to whom the data may be disclosed

If the data subject believes that data recorded about them are inaccurate the person may apply to the court, for an order which may require that the inaccurate data, and any expression of opinion based on it, is rectified, blocked, erased or destroyed.

The Data Protection Act 1998 requires every data controller who is processing personal data to notify the Information Commissioner's Office unless they are exempt. Failure to notify is a criminal offence. However, data controllers who only process personal data for staff administration are exempt from notifying.

Companies may set out their own policies on confidentiality. For example, they may require that computer screens are switched off if the user is not at their workstation, or they may restrict access to certain offices which contain sensitive information.


**Maintaining Accounting Records**

**The Companies Act 2006** is the law relating to limited companies. This is a mammoth piece of legislation with 1300 sections. Sections 380-474 cover accounts and reports. It states that 'the directors of every company must prepare accounts for the company for each of its financial years'

The Act states

1. Every company must keep adequate accounting records.

2. Adequate accounting records means records that are sufficient:-

    a. to show and explain the company's transactions,

    b. to disclose with reasonable accuracy, at any time, the financial position of the company at that time, and
    c. to enable the directors to ensure that any accounts required to be prepared comply with the requirements of this Act

3.  Accounting records must, in particular, contain:-

    a.  entries from day to day, of all sums of money received and expended by the company and the matters in respect of which the receipt and expenditure takes place, and

    b.  a record of the assets and liabilities of the company.

4.  If the company's business involves dealing in goods, the accounting records must contain:-

    a.  statements of stock held by the company at the end of each financial year of the company,

    b.  all statements of stocktakings from which any statement of stock as is mentioned in paragraph (a), has been or is to be prepared, and

    c.  except in the case of goods sold by way of ordinary retail trade, statements of all goods sold and purchased, showing the goods and the buyers and sellers in sufficient detail to enable all these to be identified.

The Act also stipulates what accounts must be kept.

A company's individual accounts may be prepared in accordance with section 396 ("Companies Act individual accounts")

    a)  a balance sheet as at the last day of the financial year, and
    b)  a profit and loss account.

Basically a balance sheet is a statement of what the company owns and what the company owes. A profit and loss account is a statement of income and expenditure for the year.

They can also include two further primary statements, being that of the cash flow statement (which shows how changes in balance sheet accounts and income affect cash) and the statement of total recognised gains and losses (which shows items not on the balance sheet or profit and loss account such as property revaluation or gains and losses by way of foreign currency transactions).

Alternatively a company may prepare financial statements in accordance with international accounting standards (IAS). These differ from the above in terminology and small differences in what is reported and how. (The IAS financial statements are covered in the AAT's Financial Statements unit at level 4).

# CHAPTER 3
## Company Policies and Procedures

The Act requires that directors of a company must send their annual accounts to **Companies House**. This is an agency of the government and is where all companies must register when they are formed. There are strict deadlines for filing of company accounts. If the shares of a company are offered for sale to the general public (a **public limited company or plc**), the accounts must be filed six months after the end of the accounting period. If the shares are not offered for sale to the general public (a **private limited company**) the accounts must be filed nine months after the end of the accounting period. If the filing is late the company will face a fine of between £150 and £7500, depending on how late the accounts are filed. Repeat late filing will result in the fine being doubled. Those companies which are quoted on an official list as having shares for sale must also make their annual accounts available on a website.

Every year the company must circulate the financial accounts (or in some cases a summary of the financial accounts) to each shareholder. An annual general meeting (AGM) must be held each year where the accounts are approved by the shareholders.

Businesses which are not limited companies (such as sole traders) have much less regulation. Such businesses are not required to prepare formal accounts as limited companies are. However, they must still keep a record of income and expenditure over a set **accounting period**, usually 12 months. This information is required by HMRC so that the correct tax can be calculated.

**Ordering goods and services**

There are no legal requirements for ordering goods or services apart from the fact that records must be kept. Each organisation is therefore free to make its own regulations. Very small companies may not have a written procedure, but where employees have a certain amount of autonomy, it is vital.

Certain people within the organisation will be given the authority to order goods. In larger organisation there may be several people authorised to make orders who have responsibility for a certain type of goods or a certain value of goods. These are often referred to as **budget holders**. Budget holders can delegate the ordering process, but the budget holder must authorise the purchase.

Depending on the complexity and size of an organisation, the following documents may be used to order goods. Not all documents are used by all businesses, and some may only use one – the invoice. However, in all but the very smallest of businesses, a written procedures document should be produced.

The documents which may be used are:

- **A purchase order**

  A document will be sent to the supplier requesting the goods. It must be signed by the budget holder or some other person in authority named in the policy. For large orders, two signatures may be required.

- **A delivery note**

  A delivery note may be received with the goods when they arrive. Remember there will be at least two copies of this; one for the buyer and one for the seller. The delivery note will be signed by a suitable person and becomes proof that the buyer has received the goods.

- **A goods received note**

  This is a document used by some companies to tell the receiving staff (probably the stores manager) what is expected on the deliveries.

---

**DAWSON SUPPLIES**

45 Scartho Street, Immingham, IM15 2BH

**Goods Received Note**

From:     **Halls Ltd**

| Description of item(s) | Quantity | Received in good condition? |
|---|---|---|
| Blue Cotton Dress Material | 50 rolls | |
| | | |
| | | |

Signed                                                    Date:

---

You can see that the goods received note is an internal document. The goods expected will already appear on the document. It is up to the receiving person to complete the 'Received in good condition?' boxes and to sign and date it. It will be used by the accounts department as a check that the correct goods have been received and that they are in good condition so that the invoice can be paid when the time comes.

- **An invoice**

    The buyer will receive an invoice from the seller sometimes at the same time as the goods are delivered, but more usually in the post a day or so later. Some companies pay invoices when they receive the statement while others will pay after the maximum number of days allowed. It's important that purchase invoices are checked for accuracy of both what goods have been charged for and the amount charged for them.

You can see the importance authorisation is given to these documents. Authorising documents is a vital part of ensuring the business runs smoothly and efficiently. It ensures that goods are not ordered unnecessarily. It ensures that problems or errors can be dealt with by the correct person swiftly and efficiently. It ensures that goods are only bought within the restrictions of the budget so that the business does not spend more than it can afford.

It is vital, therefore, that everyone knows what needs authorising and by whom. We have seen in chapter 1 how a business needs an orgainsational structure. This organisational structure is also important in showing who is responsible for authorising what. Employees should be fully familiar with the ordering process and who can authorise what. In all but the smallest of businesses, this can only be done with a policies and procedures document.

## Making payments

We saw in Chapter 2 the need for solvency. Ensuring a business is solvent means that a company has sufficient working capital to pay its debts when they become due. The important phrase here is 'when they become due'.

Debts must be paid, but if they are paid at the wrong time the business may become short of funds.

Paying late can have serious consequences. It can result in fines, legal action against the company, and even a winding up order in the most serious of cases. This is quite apart from the bad reputation which it will create, with the possible consequences of the supplier refusing to trade with the company. Late payment of taxes to HMRC invariably results in a fine. In serious cases the fine can be very large and has been known to lead to a business going bankrupt or going into liquidation.

Early payment can also have serious consequenses. An organisation which has negotiated (say) 30 days credit with a supplier has done so to aid cash flow. The ultimate aim is to reduce the time between paying the supplier for the goods and receiving payment from the customer. If you then pay the supplier early you will reduce the working capital, and run the risk of becoming insolvent. Settlement (cash) discounts are sometimes offered by suppliers to encourage early payment. The customer must decide whether the discount should be taken. If paying early to take advantage of the reduced price means that borrowing from the bank will be required, it may not benefit the company. A decision on settlement discounts should be taken by senior members of the business.

It is vital, therefore, that the company has a policy on making payments. Invoices should be paid strictly according to the policy and they should be authorised for payment. Remember that you should **never** pay an invoice until you are authorised to do so. Many companies will either have someone to sign the invoice ready for payment or it will be rubber stamped. Whatever the method, you should be aware of when invoices are paid and who authorises them for payment.

Cheques are often signed at the same time as the invoice is authorised for payment. Senior members of staff usually have responsibility for signing cheques. The cheque sometimes requires two or more signatures. More often than not the cheque is prepared by a junior member of staff but signed by a senior member.

Rules for handling cash are of particular importance. The contents of a till will be checked at least daily with the till roll, preferably by someone who is not responsible for putting the money in the till in the first place. Cash should be bank as soon as possible. Cash should be taken to the bank daily, or if this is impossible it should be kept in a safe. Relatively small amounts should be taken to the bank by two people – not someone on their own. Larger amounts should be taken by a security firm who will vary their route and time.

Small amounts of cash may be kept on the premises to cover small items such as tea, stamps or envelopes. This is called petty cash. Rules will be made on how much should be kept and a limit on the amount which can be used for each transaction. A system of vouchers is often in place so that a record of the expenses paid can be kept. Payments made from petty cash should be authorised. A check will be made on the amount of notes and coins in the petty cash tin daily.

Again, it can be seen that efficiency in the workplace is achieved by a company policy and more importantly, by a system of authorisation. What payments can be made is set down in writing and regulated by a designated person. In this way payments are kept under control and problems and errors can be address to the person in charge immediately.

## VAT

Value Added Tax (VAT) is a tax on buying and selling and, along with income tax, is the most important way the government gets its income. Businesses registered for VAT must charge the tax on all the goods they sell (with a few exceptions which are covered in the VAT book available from this publisher). The rate in the UK is currently 20%.

When a business reaches (or is expected to reach) a turnover (i.e. total value of all sales in a year) of £77,000, then that business must register for VAT. This amount changes usually annually so you should check at www.hmrc.gov.uk at least once a year. If a business fails to register for VAT when they should, HMRC will impose a fine as well as reclaiming the VAT which should have been charged. Businesses have been known to become insolvent because they cannot afford the penalties. Once a business registers for VAT the business must legally create invoices following the regulations shown below.

# CHAPTER 3
## Company Policies and Procedures

When a VAT registered trader sells goods to another VAT registered trader then a VAT invoice **must** be supplied within 30 days of the sale. Buyers can only claim back any VAT paid if they hold a valid VAT invoice. You don't need to give a VAT invoice if you are the retailer unless the customer asks for one. This means that when you go to the shop to buy goods for your own use, the shop doesn't need to give you a VAT invoice unless you ask for one. It is illegal to issue a VAT invoice unless you are registered.

A VAT invoice must show the following:

- an invoice number which is unique and follows on from the number of the previous invoice - if you spoil or cancel a serially numbered invoice, you must keep it to show to a VAT officer at your next VAT inspection.

- the seller's name or trading name, and address.

- the seller's VAT registration number. This number is given to the trader when he/she registers for VAT.

- the invoice date.

- the time of supply (also known as tax point) if this is different from the invoice date - see later in this chapter.

- the customer's name or trading name, and address.

- a description sufficient to identify the goods or services supplied to the customer.

- unit price or rate, excluding VAT. (The cost of each item without VAT).

- quantity of goods or the extent of the services (for example 12 reams of paper or 6 hours of accountancy time).

- rate of VAT that applies to what's being sold.

- total amount payable, excluding VAT .

- rate of any cash discount .

- total amount of VAT charged (but you don't need to show the VAT amount for each individual item).

- If you supply zero rated or exempt goods or services on the same invoice then you must show clearly that there is no VAT payable and the total value of these goods must be shown separately.

- The total charge made including VAT.

A VAT registered business is required by law to keep records of their taxable transactions. As long as records are kept clearly then any layout is acceptable although HMRC do make recommendations and provide examples (see the book 'Value Added Tax' by the same author).

A VAT return must be made by all VAT registered businesses. A return must usually be made every three months. This is now usually completed online. A return will show the VAT charged on sales and the VAT paid on purchases. The amount is netted off and a payment is made to or from HMRC. In most cases a VAT returns must be submitted by one month and 7 days after the period to which they apply. A penalty will be imposed if it is late.

VAT officers will visit businesses from time to time to check that the VAT records are being kept correctly, that VAT is being charged correctly and that only the VAT on eligible purchases are reclaimed.

You can see that keeping the financial records accurate and up to date is essential for the efficiency and solvency of a business.

**Payroll processing**

A business is required by law to keep full and accurate payroll records for each employee for the current and previous three tax years. These must include:

- a record of their name and address

- payslips or some other record showing their gross earnings, and the tax and National Insurance Contributions deducted.

HMRC may ask to see evidence of how the calculations for any of these are made. They may also ask to see supporting information like invoices and receipts.

As with VAT, officers will visit businesses from time to time to check that the payroll records are being kept correctly. If they are not, HMRC can impose a fine.

Every employer must file an annual return for the payroll records (a P14 and a P35). This must be submitted by 19th May each year. Again, a fine will be imposed if it is late.
Once again keeping the payroll records accurate and up to date is essential for the efficiency and solvency of a business.

**Retaining documents**

Legally there are differing instructions on how long accounting documents are to be kept. The **Companies Act 2006** states that a public limited company must keep records for six years from the date they are drawn up. Since the accounting records are made up for the year, some documentation from the beginning of the year will need to be kept, which in effect will make it seven years.

The **Companies Act 2006** states that private limited companies must keep similar records for three years.

The **Finance Act 1997** amended the requirement in the **Value Added Tax Act 1994** so that accounting records for VAT should be kept for six years.

**The Income Tax (Pay As You Earn) Regulations 2003** states that employers must keep payroll records for not less than three years.

The **Limitations Act 1980** requires that any action for a contract or fraud expires after six years. However, documents may be required for longer if such action is taken within the six years.

The **Taxes Management Act 1970** says that an assessment for tax can be made up to six years after the end of the period to which it relates, but personal tax documents need only be kept for 1 year and 10 months.

The **Data Protection Act** states that personal data processed for any purpose or purposes shall not be kept for longer than is necessary for that purpose or those purposes.

Other legislation requires certain documents to be retained for between 1 year and permanently.

So you can see that the legislation is confusing. It is therefore essential that the business has a policy on document retention. For most accounting documents this is often 6 years after the end of the period to which it relates. In most cases this will be sufficient to cover all possible claims made by employees, HMRC or customers. If documents are not available when they should be a fine will be imposed.

# CHAPTER 3
## Company Policies and Procedures

**'Green' issues**

With environmental issues becoming more and more dominant, many companies are producing policies for saving energy and other resources. Some business sectors have strict regulations on reducing pollution, particularly the oil and chemical industries. In an office environment, 'green' policies are largely voluntary.

A business may have a policy and procedures document to cover items such as those shown below:

Paper – An office may aim to reduce the use of paper. In fact some offices are now 'paperless' whereby all documentation is stored electronically. Those offices which must use paper may seek to buy recycled and will recycle paper wherever possible. The business may seek to reduce the amount of packaging on its products and amy also aim to buy products which have little or no packaging.

Cleaning – The choice of cleaning materials may based on environmental issues as well as cost. Cleaning practices may be monitored to avoid excessive amounts of cleaning mixtures entering the waste disposal system

Energy – Lights and electrical equipment should be switched off when not in use. Heating may be adjusted so that the temperature is comfortable and not warm. Energy consumption may be taken into consideration when buying new equipment.

Office Equipment – Evaluation of the need of certain items of equipment may be made to see if the need can be met in another way. Renting or sharing equipment may be considered before purchasing. Selling or recycling old or unwanted equipment may be considered.

Transportation – Business trips may be restricted and alternatives (such as email or video conferencing) may be considered. The use of public transport or bicycles to get to work may be promoted. Only vehicles with low $CO_2$ emissions may be purchased for the company or even electric vehicles may be considered.

Whatever the company decides should be written in a policy document.

**Company procedures**

In all but the very smallest of businesses, a written policy and procedures document should be available. We have seen that some policies are required by law, but more often than not, managers and employers will have policies which exceed the minimum legal requirement.

Policies and procedures are fundamental to the success of a business. They ensure a safe and efficient workplace. Wherever possible they should be drawn up in consultation with all staff and they should be reviewed at least annually.

# CHAPTER 3
## Company Policies and Procedures

If all staff are following the same rules and regulations, the business will be effective, safe and efficient.

---

**Chapter Summary**

- Policies and procedures are fundamental to the success of a business.

- A policy document will be produced by all but the smallest of business to cover all aspects of workplace activities.

- Some policies are required by law, while others may be added to further improve the efficiency of the business

- A code of conduct will be drawn up by the business to ensure that the staff meets the minimum standards of behaviour expected by the business.

- The safety of the workplace is required by law. It is primarily covered by **The Health and Safety at Work Act 1974.**

- Confidentiality of personal information is covered by **The Data Protection Act 1998.** A business may also extend confidentiality to some or all of its working practices.

- Businesses are required by law to maintain certain accounting information.

- A policy on how and when to order goods should be made so that goods can be ordered before stocks run out and also in order to keep within budget.

- A policy on how and when to make payments should be made to ensure the solvency of the business.

- Businesses are required by law to retain documents. For how long should be stated in the company policy.

- A business may draw up a policy for being environmentally friendly.

---

# **Practice Questions**

## **Chapter 3**

**3.1**

Which of the following statements best describes a policies and procedures document?

a)      A document explaining the laws covering the workplace.

b)      A document which must be displayed in the workplace covering Health & Safety.

c)      A document explaining the rules and regulations for all workplace activities.

d)      A rule book showing how employees should conduct themselves in the office.

**3.2**

Which of the following statements best describes a code of conduct?

a)      A document explaining the laws covering the workplace.

b)      A document which must be displayed in the workplace covering Health & Safety.

c)      A document explaining the rules and regulations for all workplace activities.

d)      A rule book showing how employees should conduct themselves in the office.

**3.3**

Which of the following best describes a Health & Safety policy statement?

a)      A set of rules restricting the activities of employees.

b)      A set of rules ensuring you look after you own safety.

c)      A set of rules drawn up by the employer to ensure the health and safety of employees and others in the workplace.

d)      A set of rules issued by the government to ensure safety in the workplace.

**3.4**

Why is confidentiality required in the workplace?

a)      So that personal information on employees is not seen by anyone except those authorised to do so.

b)      So that competitors don't obtain sensitive information on the business's working practices.

c)      So that customers can remain anonymous if they wish.

d)      So that others don't find out how much you earn unless you want them to know.

**3.5**

Which of the following statements are true?

a)      All businesses must keep records of income and expenditure.

b)      All businesses must produce a Profit & Loss account (Income Statement).

c)      The financial accounts of limited companies are confidential.

d)      All businesses must employ an accountant to draw up the financial statements.

**3.6**

Which of the following statements are true?

a)      All accounting documents must be destroyed after 6 years.

b)      All documents containing personal details must be destroyed after 6 years.

c)      All documents containing personal details can be kept permanently if the business wishes.

d)      There are no documents which can be kept permanently.

**3.7**

Which of the following statements are true?

a)     All businesses must charge VAT on their sales.

b)     All businesses must give an invoice to their customers.

c)     All VAT registered businesses must give an invoice to their customers if they request one.

d)     All businesses registered for VAT must send a return to HMRC annually.

**3.8**

Which of the following statements are true?

a)     All payments should be authorized.

b)     It is a legal requirement that payments should be authorized.

c)     Only payments by cheque need be authorized.

d)     Only payments by cash need be authorized.

**3.9**

Which of the following statements are true?

a)     All invoices should be paid as soon as possible.

b)     The payment of all invoices should be delayed as long as possible.

c)     A company policy should indicate when invoices are to be paid.

d)     A business should always take advantage of a settlement (cash) discount if one is offered.

**3.10**

Which of the following statements are true?

a)      All businesses are required by law to have a policy on environmental issues.

b)      There are no laws governing environmental issues.

c)      The company policy on environmental issues should encourage employees to use public transport to get to work.

d)      The company policy on environmental issues should encourage employees to recycle materials.

This page is for your notes

# Chapter 4

## Ethics and Sustainability

In this chapter we will be looking at ethics in business. We will see how ethical behaviour can bring benefits to a business. We will look at the fundamental principles of ethics in accounting. We will also look at sustainability; what it is and why it is important in business.

Ethics in business is about doing the right thing. The business should be not only fair and honest, but also be seen to be fair and honest.

Business ethics was mentioned as long ago as 350BC in Aristotle's 'Politics', but has developed most in the period from the early 1970's. Ethical businesses apply principles of honesty and fairness in relationships with co-workers and customers.

Some people believe that acting ethically increases costs, but today this is seen as short-sighted. Unethical behaviour may be seen as the shortest route to greatest profits but the damage it can cause to a business's reputation will have long-term repercussions, resulting in the loss of customers and potential investors and shareholders.

Ethical behaviour can bring significant benefits to a business. It can:

- Attract customers to the business's products, thereby increasing sales and profits

- Make employees want to stay with the business, reducing labour turnover and increasing productivity

- Attract more employees to the business, reducing recruitment costs and attracting the most talented people to the business.

- Attract investors, which will keep share prices high and help to prevent unwanted takeovers.

Many businesses will have a written Code of Ethics. The code will determine how employees or members of a profession (including the AAT) should behave. A Code of Ethics will not only affect how the employee or member acts in the workplace, but it will also extend to behaviour outside the workplace. The interests of the business or profession should be upheld even when with family or friends.

# CHAPTER 4
## Ethics and Sustainability

**Fundamental Principles**

All accounting professionals are expected to act in the public interest and to promote high ethical and technical standards. However, when dealing with the financial affairs of a company or individual, there can be occasions where the needs of the business are in conflict with the public interest. There have been recent high profile examples of this whereby the accountants have taken the interests of the business by explaining how to economise on tax costs, which at the same time deprives the public purse of funds by avoiding tax. (Tax avoidance is legal; tax evasion is not).

The accounting profession, including the AAT, have five fundamental ethical principles. You will need to memorise these.

- **Integrity**

  This is about being honest, truthful, straightforward and having strong moral principles.

- **Objectivity**

  This is about not being influenced by personal feelings or opinions in considering or representing the facts. It is also about representing the facts as they are without the undue influence of others.

- **Professional Competence and Due Care**

  This is about maintaining professional knowledge and skill and keeping up with new developments, legislation and techniques to ensure that the client or employer receives the best possible service. It is also about not acting recklessly and without due consideration of the facts.

- **Confidentiality**

  This is about keeping information acquired as a result of business activities, secret. Such information should not be used for personal gain, or disclosed to anyone else without explicit permission to disclose it, or where there is a legal requirement to disclose it.

- **Professional Behaviour**

  This is about acting in a professional way (both in the workplace and outside), being a law-abiding citizen, and not bringing the accountancy profession into disrepute.

There is a further ethical principle you should learn – equality.

- **Equality**

    This is about men and women, people of different races, religions, etc. all being treated fairly and having the same opportunities.

## Integrity

Integrity is basing one's actions on a framework of principles. It consists of obeying the rules and doing the right thing. This isn't always as easy as it may seem. There may be pressures to breach your integrity. Doing the wrong thing might be brought about by external pressures. For example your boss may ask you to falsify some figures. You know you may lose your job if you don't agree. But a person with integrity will not agree to do wrong. They will refuse to falsify facts no matter what the consequences.

It may seem that power, fortune and success can be gained instantly if corners are cut and the constraints of moral principles are forgotten, but to build a reputation of integrity takes years, and you can lose it in a second.

We live in a world where we believe the end justifies the means. It may be tempting to overstate profits so that investors will put their money into the business. We may think there is nothing wrong with calling in 'sick' when in actual fact all we want to do is go Christmas shopping. How tempting is it to add a few miles onto the business travelling so we can get a few extra expenses out of the business? In every case the person committing the act of dishonesty will convince themselves that they had a perfectly valid reason for their lack of integrity. However, this temporary monetary profit comes at a great price. Any trust can be lost forever.

The value of integrity is far beyond anything that can be measured. For people in business it means that investors will trust them when investing their capital, and customers will come again and again to buy their goods with confidence. For employees it means that the manager or boss will be willing to trust them with additional responsibilities. For the accountant it will mean that the client can trust that the advice they are given will be fair, straightforward and honest.

Integrity applies equally to large and small matters. It applies to the recording of financial statements, where figures must not be misleading or inaccurate, and it applies to the expense claims for tea and coffee for the staff where the amounts must be accurate and genuine.

# CHAPTER 4
## Ethics and Sustainability

**Objectivity**

Objectivity is basing an opinion on the facts only, without personal opinions, stereotypes or based on the opinions of others. For example, if you describe an object objectively you can state its colour, size and weight, but as soon as you say the object is ugly you are no longer objective. Whether it is ugly is based on personal opinion.

The principle behind objectivity is that if two separate accountants were asked to give advice on a particular topic, they would both come up with the same answer. If your managing director believes a particular asset is worth £50,000 but a professional valuation gives the price as £40,000, the asset should be recorded at £40,000. The £40,000 is objective because it is supported by a professional appraisal and is not subject to the managing director's personal opinion.

There are two basic ways objectivity can be threatened

### 1. Conflict of interest

A conflict of interest is any situation that might cause an impartial observer to reasonably question whether your actions are influenced by considerations of private interests. 'Private interests' can include financial interests, interests related to your personal relationships, or interests related to other outside activities. For example, you may suggest that a contract is given to a company in which you have a substantial shareholding. Because you have a personal financial interest in the result, your professional judgement may be (or be seen to be) influenced by the situation rather than based solely on the facts.

Conflicts of interest can influence a decision either deliberately or accidentally. You may be faced with a situation where a close friend or family member is interviewed for a new job where you are involved in the hiring. Your objective opinion may be influenced.

You may be involved with another organisation which offers the same or similar services. If you are an employee of one accounting business and offer a similar service as a sole trader to similar clients you may be influenced in your judgement.

A conflict of interest exists whether or not the individual is actually influenced by the circumstances. It exists where the circumstances are reasonably believed to *create a risk* that decisions will be influenced.

Soliciting or accepting excessive gifts or hospitality is a common way in which a conflict of interest can arise. Accepting an occasional gift is acceptable where the gift is unsolicited, modest in value and provided openly. What is modest in value is not specified, but a bottle of wine at Christmas is acceptable but an all expenses paid holiday to Bermuda is not. If you accept an expensive gift it may cloud your judgment and influence your advice or decision.

There are two ways to overcome a conflict of interest. You should either refuse the engagement, or you should declare the interest to the organisation or client when the decision is made.

## 2. Undue influence

This is where professional judgement will be affected due to one person's position of power over another person. For example, you may be told to report something that isn't true otherwise you will be overlooked for promotion. You should not be influenced in this way. If possible you should report this to a senior person in the company. If this has no effect, you should accept you will be overlooked and seek alternative employment. The business is acting unethically if not illegally and they are most likely to be found out at some time. You don't want to be implicit in the unethical activity. This can have an even greater detrimental effect on your future career than not getting the promotion.

## Professional Competence and Due Care

Professional Competence is about maintaining professional skills and knowledge at a level to ensure that employers and clients receive a competent service. Continuing Professional Development (CPD) is the means by which people maintain their knowledge and skills. This topic is covered in detail in Chapter 10.

Due care is to act diligently in accordance with the technical and professional standards required by the service offered. There is a requirement to carry out the task or tasks carefully, thoroughly and on time. There is also a duty to make

Where appropriate you should make clients and employers aware of any limitatiions in the service offered and you should refuse to carry out any tasks which for which you are not technically competent.

A breach of duty of care can occur where you are trying to carry out tasks whithout checking your facts and figures, either through negligence or through a lack of time.

A breach of professional competence will occur where you are trying to carry out tasks for which you have little knowledge or where you have not kept up to date with recent developments. For example, you must not offer tax as a service if you havn't studied tax for the past five years. Similarly you must refuse to carry out tasks on inheritance tax if you haven't studied inheritance tax.

CHAPTER 4
Ethics and Sustainability

**Confidentiality**

An accountant has a responsibility to act in the client's (or employer's) best interest. This cannot be achieved if the client (or employer) believes that the information given to the accountant will be shared with others. Therefore an accountant has a duty not to disclose any confidential information acquired as a result of professional and business relationships without the specific authority of the client (or employer). An accountant must also refrain from using confidential information for personal gain.

The duty of not disclosing confidential information is not confined to customers, clients and suppliers. You should take steps to ensure that this information is not accidentally disclosed in social situations or to family members. For example you must take care not to talk about a client's affairs at the gym, restaurant, or on family outings. Even sharing information with work colleagues can be a breach of confidentiality.

Confidential information can take many forms. For example you may find out that your client is considering taking over a competitor, or you may know the phone number of your client. It doesn't matter how material the information is, you must still keep the information secure and private.

You should take care that you do not disclose information inadvertently. You should never reveal information over the telephone. You can't be sure who is at the other end of the line. There are also organisations that collect information for statistical purposes. Never reveal information to marketing and data collection agencies without the express permission of the client or employer.

The principle of confidentiality continues even after the individual has left the employment or after the relationship with the client has ended. You cannot go to a new job and tell the new employer confidential information about your previous employment.

There are occasions where disclosure of confidential information is permitted. There are broadly three situations where disclosure is permitted.

1. When the client has given permission. An example might be when a client wishes to obtain a loan and the bank or lender has asked for certain financial information from the client. The accountant may be given permission to disclose this information on behalf of the client. An accountant will also need the consent of the client to reveal information to Her Majesty's Revenue and Customs in any tax matters. However, the consent must be explicit and an accountant would be wise to get the permission in writing.

2. When there is a legal duty to disclose the information. An example might be when the accountant suspects the client is committing fraud. The Fraud Act 2006 states that disclosure of such information is a legal requirement.

3. When there is a professional duty to disclose information. An example might be to protect the professional interests of a professional accountant in legal proceedings. There

may also be a public interest reason for disclosing information. An example might be where the client's activities will cause substantial environmental damage.

Keeping personal data confidential is required by law under the Data Protection Act. This act is covered on p34 to p35 of this book.

## Professional Behaviour

Accountants have an obligation to comply with relevant laws and avoid any actions that will bring the accounting profession into disrepute. Accountants must not take part in any 'shady' deals, and they must not 'bend the rules' to accommodate their client's wishes.

Professional Behaviour extends to how you portray yourself as an accountant. You cannot say you are a chartered accountant if you are not. You must also be careful when marketing your business. Advertising material must be truthful and should not make exaggerated claims. Advertising should not make disparaging references or unsubstantiated comparisons with other businesses. You cannot say that you will guarantee to reduce the client's tax bill because this will depend on the client's previous financial activities. You can say that you will ensure the client will pay only what is due.

You cannot say that you are better than the rest. You don't state what exactly you are better at, and in any case you don't have any substantiated evidence that you are better than the rest.

## Equality

Equality in the workplace can be defined as treating everyone the same regardless of age, race, sex, sexual orientation, religion, national origin or physical disability. All workers are entitled to be held in the same esteem as any of the co-worker. Equality is supported in law by the Equality Act 2010. Equality applies not only to employees and co-workers, but also to customers and suppliers.

An employer cannot seek a 'young person', or a 'male person' without a genuine reason for this. Employers must also avoid stereotypes. You cannot overlook a woman for what has traditionally been a male dominated job, or vice versa. A woman may be just as good a bricklayer as a man may be a manicurist.

Equality covers all areas of the workplace. Recruitment cannot ask for a British person and you cannot pay a man more than a woman for doing the same job.

# CHAPTER 4
## Ethics and Sustainability

**Sustainability**

The 2005 World Summit on Social Development identified 'three pillars' of sustainability. These are the 3 E's:

- Economic development

- Environmental protection

- Social equity

All three of the above are types of sustainability.

**Economic development**

This involves supporting ways for people to create wealth without harming natural systems or human beings. Sustainable economic growth means a rate of growth that can be maintained without creating other significant problems.

Rapid growth today may exhaust resources and create environmental problems in the future. For example rapid growth in the fishing industry may cause problems in the future with depleted fish stocks. Increased demand for fuel oils will cause problems with oil resources for future generations.

In order to maintain sustainable economic growth it is necessary to find alternative energy sources, reduce the spiralling growth of the economy and contain the increasing depletion of resources.

**Environmental protection**

While economic development is more a global problem, environmental protection can be carried out at the individual level. Many businesses will have a 'green' policy (see p44). The principle purpose of a 'green' policy is to

- Reduce the 'carbon footprint'. Businesses will reduce their $CO_2$ emissions with cycle to work policies or only using electric or low emission vehicles.

- Recycle as much as possible. Many businesses now require waste to be collected in separate groups. Paper, plastic and cardboard can all be recycled. In addition the business may encourage the purchase of goods that have been recycled such as paper, glass and plastic.

- Reduce energy consumption. Businesses may encourage low energy lighting and will try to ensure that energy is not wasted by turning off lights when not needed.

# CHAPTER 4
## Ethics and Sustainability

### The cost of sustainability

In the past one of the barriers to adopting sustainability was the cost. It has been seen that sustainability can sometimes cost more than the traditional way of doing things. For example, there are costs involved with recycling.

- There are the costs of providing 'green' facilities such as more bins and for taking the separate types of rubbish away.

- The cost of low energy lighting is generally higher than traditional lighting.

- Many environmentally friendly products cost more than traditional products. Electric cars, for example cost more than traditional petrol or diesel cars.

- There are costs involved with modifying products so they are environmentally friendly.

However, there is a trade-off. If you buy low energy lighting there will be lower electricity bills. If you buy fuel-efficient vehicles you will have lower fuel costs and save on tax.

There is also the unseen cost of not 'going green'. 'Green' products are easier to sell and are less likely to become obsolete. We have seen that not using sustainable resources will result in shortages of products such as fossil fuels in the future. Scarce recourses mean they will cost more.

### Social equity

Social equity can be defined as equal opportunity in a safe and healthy environment, and is the third branch of sustainability.

Many businesses have realised that looking after its staff has the economic benefit of staff retention and improved efficiency. A happy employee will work harder and more efficiently than an unhappy one. Businesses will therefore provide opportunities for the staff to 'bond'. They will provide activities and entertainment outside of work time or even on occasions in work time. Some businesses provide gyms and clubs for their workers. It will also benefit the business if the employee is provided with vocational training.

The business will benefit from being involved with the local community. A business which sponsors local events will reap the reward of increasing customers. Some businesses will even organise local events or sponsor the local football team.

Many businesses will raise funds for charities, such as Children in Need or Oxfam. They may sponsor national sports or arts events. Examples are the Sainsbury Athletics Championship, and the Barclays Premier League.

# CHAPTER 4
## Ethics and Sustainability

**Corporate Social Responsibility (CSR)**

Attention to ethical issues is increasingly common in boardrooms. Social responsibility is seen as characterising the 'right way' to run a business as well as being essential for long term success. Businesses see their success tied to the success of their communities. When a business promotes itself as being socially responsible it is known as **Corporate Social Responsibility (CSR)**.

Corporate Social Responsibility can benefit a business in the following ways:

- A CSR programme can aid staff recruitment and retention. Potential recruits will often ask about a business's CSR policy at interview.

- A CSR programme can reduce, or at least offset, damage to reputation by such incidents as corruption scandals or environmental accidents. BP, for instance, has a very active and high profile CSR programme which to a certain extent relieves the damage to the good name of the business brought about by the disastrous environmental damage which it caused in the Gulf of Mexico in April 2010.

- Companies strive for a unique selling position that can separate them from the competition in the minds of consumers. CSR can play a role in building customer loyalty.

- Businesses may seek suppliers who can prove their products come from sustainable sources, or use environmentally safe methods in their production. You may be familiar with the use of the Fairtrade label. Fairtrade is a social movement that ensures disadvantaged farmers and workers in developing countries get a better deal through the use of the international Fairtrade Mark. There are several Fairtrade certifies throughout the world.

- Finding the cheapest price is no longer what always matters most to consumers. Instead they expect companies to operate in a socially responsible manner. The 2013 Cone Communications/Echo Global CSR Study found that more than eight-in-10 consider CSR when deciding where to work (81%), what to buy or where to shop (87%) and which products and services to recommend to others (85%).

Types of CSR include:

- Reducing the 'carbon footprint'. $CO_2$ emissions can be reduced by large or small programmes. A policy of switching off lights when not needed can reduce $CO_2$ as can curbing pollution or even developing 'clean' energy.

- Businesses may donate to local or national charities. They may give time or money to local community programmes.

- Businesses will treat employees fairly and ethically. They may provide comprehensive training and promotion prospects.

There are many examples of CSR in large companies.

- The Body Shop has made a stand against animal testing since 1985.

- Starbucks focuses on sustainable production of 'green' coffee.

- Ben and Jerry's donate 7.5% of pretax profits to charities.

- Pedigree sponsors animal shelters and it aims to donate 4 million bowls of dog food to these shelters.

These are just a few examples of Corporate Social Responsibility in action today.

---

**Chapter Summary**

- Ethical behaviour can bring benefits to a business.

- There are six ethical principles for accountants
  Integrity
  Objectivity
  Professional Competence and Due Care
  Confidentiality
  Professional Behaviour
  Equality

- There are three pillars of sustainability
  Economic development
  Environmental protection
  Social equity

- Businesses are increasingly promoting Corporate Social Responsibility (CSR)

# **Practice Questions**

## **Chapter 4**

**4.1**

Which of the following are among the five fundamental ethical principles for the accountancy profession.

a)      Integrity

b)      Confidentiality

c)      Professional Behaviour

d)      Honesty

e)      Truthfulness

f)      Professional competence and due care

g)      Social Responsibility

h)      Sustainability

**4.2**

Match the following statements to the fundamental principles

a)      You should be straightforward & honest when carrying out your professional duties.

b)      You should maintain & uphold the good reputation of the accountancy profession and not bring any discredit to it.

c)      You should base your decisions on facts & not allow any personal prejudice, bias or pressure from others to affect that decision.

d)      When carrying out assignments you should ensure that they are always carried out with proper care & attention necessary so that the quality & standards meet the expectations of the accountancy profession.

e)      Any information gained during an assignment should not be disclosed to anyone without proper authority.

f)     You should ensure that you are sufficiently competent in terms of skills & experience before carrying out work assigned to you.


**4.3**

Which of the following scenarios will breach a fundamental principle? If it does breach one of the principles state which one.

| Scenario | Breach of principle (Yes/No) | Principle Breached |
|---|---|---|
| The business you work for wants a new trainee and has advertised for a person under the age of 25. | | |
| Your brother has just started a new business selling stationery to local businesses. You suggest that your company uses this business but you don't tell them that the owner is your brother. | | |
| A friend of yours has just been told that she is to inherit a substantial amount of money from a long lost relative who has just died. Your friend asks if you will deal with the inheritance tax details. You don't know much about inheritance tax but you agree because she is your friend. | | |
| You suspect that one of your clients is using the profits from his business to fund terrorist activities. You tell the police of your suspicions. | | |
| You are keen to get the job advertised in the jobs pages of an internet site. You decide to amend your CV to say that you are AAT qualified even though you have still to complete the last two units. | | |
| Your boss asks you to understate the value of stock held in the warehouse in order to artificially reduce the profit shown in the Statement of Profit or Loss. You refuse | | |

**4.4**

Which of the following statements are true?

a)      Sustainability involves selling cheap, inferior goods to make most profit

b)      Sustainability involves seeking materials and products from suppliers where the employees are paid a fair wage even though these may be more expensive than from another supplier.

c)      Sustainability involves funding your staff to study for the AAT qualification

d)      Sustainability involves sponsoring local community projects so that planning permission for your new factory will go ahead more smoothly.

e)      Sustainability involves taking your staff out for a Christmas Party.


**4.5**

Which of the following are policies a business might adopt for sustainability?

a)      Having a fire drill at regular intervals.

b)      Offering work experience places for children from the local school.

c)      Putting up a notice reminding people to switch off the lights if they are the last one in the office.

d)      Keeping an accident book

e)      Putting up a Health & Safety Poster

f)      Having an annual open day for the general public.

# Chapter 5

## Working with numbers

## 1. Percentages

> Managers need to know how a business is doing year on year. This chapter deals with calculating percentages and how this can help managers with assessing how well a business's sales, costs and expenses have risen or fallen. Percentages can help with keeping costs under control and ensuring that profits are maintained.

A manager needs to know how well his business is doing so that he/she can plan for the future. Different managers will want to know different things, but overall the information should help them evaluate, control, budget, motivate, promote, celebrate, learn, and improve. Unfortunately, no single performance measure is appropriate for all eight purposes. Consequently, managers should not seek the one magic performance measure, but look at the range of measures.

Why can't we just look at the profit a company makes? Well it does tell us how much money a company makes on paper, but it doesn't help us to decide if it could have done better. It could even hide the fact that the company is in serious financial difficulties. Let us suppose that in the first month of trading your company made sales of £10,000 all of which is on credit. If the Cost of Sales was £5,000 and overheads were £2,500 we can probably see that the net profit would be (£10,000 - £5,000 - £2,500 =) £2,500. This looks like quite a healthy situation. But you will notice that all the sales are on credit. No actual money comes into the business until the debtors pay. So the situation could be that your company has spent £5,000 on materials and £2,500 on other expenses and no money has come into the business at all. The net profit of £2,500 now doesn't look so healthy, particularly if you have taken a loan to buy the materials and the bank is looking for the first instalment of the repayment. On top of this you have no money to buy further materials so that you can continue to trade. In spite of a good net profit, your business is looking at bankruptcy.

**Calculating an increase as a percentage**

Let us look at some ways in which we can judge how our company is doing. The simplest and most straightforward way is to use percentages. Percentages are useful because they make things very easy to compare. Let us take an example:

*Wilde & Co is a large company whose profits have gone up over the last two years. In 2013 it made a net profit of £1,250,000 and in 2014 it made £1,350,000.*

# CHAPTER 5
## Working with Numbers

*Sam Butler owns a small business. He too has had an increase in profits but the actual profit figure is much more modest. In 2013 his net profit was £40,000 and in 2014 it was £45,000.*

The question is whose profit has gone up the most? Well we can easily see that Wilde & Co has an increase in profit of £100,000 while Sam Butler has had an increase of £5,000. But it isn't fair to say that Wilde & Co has done better than Sam Butler because the relative size of each company makes it difficult to judge. The answer is to use a percentage.

Percentages make everything as parts of 100, no matter what the size of the actual figure. In this way we can measure the relative increase rather than the actual increase.

To calculate a percentage you take the figure divide it by what you are relating it to. Multiply this figure by 100 and you will get a percentage. Let us apply this to our example above:

*Wilde & Co's increase in profit was:*

$$£1,350,000 - £1,250,000 = £100,000$$

*We are relating this to the previous year's profit of £1,250,000.*

$$£100,000 \div £1,250,000 = 0.08$$

*Multiply the answer by 100 to get the percentage.*

$$0.08 \times 100 = 8\%$$

*This means that Wilde & Co's profits have risen by 8%.*

*Sam Butler's increase in profits was:*

$$£45,000 - £40,000 = £5,000$$

*We are relating this to the previous year's profit of £40,000.*

$$£5,000 \div £40,000 = 0.125$$

*Multiply by 100 and to get the percentage.*

$$0.125 \times 100 = 12.5\%$$

*This means that Sam Butler's profits have increased by 12.5%.*

**Relatively speaking** Sam's profits have increased more than Wilde & Co. Sam's small business has actually done better than the large company of Wilde & Co.

## Calculating a decrease as a percentage

You should remember that the same idea is used to show a percentage decrease. Let us take another example:

*Hardy Brothers sold 100,000 products in 2013, but in 2014 they only sold 98,000. We can see that they sold 2,000 fewer in 2013. Selling fewer products is always a concern, but how much of a concern can be seen more easily by a percentage.*

*2,000 fewer products are related to the 2013 figure. 2,000 ÷ 100,000 = 0.02. Multiply by 100 and we get to 2%.*

*J Swift also has had a downturn in sales. In 2013 he sold 5,000 products but in 2014 he only sold 4,500: 500 fewer in 2014 than 2013.*

*500 fewer products are related to the 2013 figure. 500 ÷ 5,000 = 0.1. Multiply by 100 and we get to 10%.*

So we can see that J Swift has had a worse time than Hardy Brothers.

> **LEARNING POINT!**
>
> Students often get percentages wrong because they forget what they are relating the figures to. A common error is to relate the increase or decrease to whatever the lower figure is. In the examples above the increase was always related to the previous year's figure. Try to remember that a percentage increase or decrease is always related to what the figure was before the increase or decrease.

Percentages are also useful for controlling costs.

*Suppose that a company has an annual wages bill of £102,720 with sales of £428,000. A similar company, selling a similar product, has a wages bill of £65,100 and sales of £310,000. Which company has the better control over wages costs?*

The difficulty in finding the answer is that the two companies have a different value of sales and, since it is a similar product, presumably a different volume of sales.

We can take away the problem of the volume by calculating the wages as a percentage of sales.

The first company has wages of £102,720 and sales of £428,000. We relate the wages to the sales and multiply by 100 to arrive at the percentage. We could, in theory, take any number, but 100 is a very simple number to deal with in calculations.

£102,720 / £428,000 x 100 = 24%

Now we do the same to the figures from the second company

£65,100 / £310,000 x 100 = 21%

So now we can see that the second company, in spite of fewer sales, has better control over wages.

**Calculating a percentage increase**

I'm sure we have all seen where prices have gone up by a certain percentage. Let us suppose that the price of a certain model of car goes up by 8%. It used to cost £7,800. What will it cost in future?

There are two methods of finding this. Method 1 is to find the actual amount the car will go up by:

£7,800 x 8% = £624 (To multiply by a percentage you can either push the % button on your calculator or divide the number by 100)

Here we can see that the extra amount that will be charged is £624, so we add this to the original price to arrive at the new price

£7,800 + £624 = £8,424.

Method 2 is the all-in-one way. The new price of the car is 108% of the old one.

£7,800 x 108% = £8,424

**How percentages can be misleading**

You must be careful with percentages and not jump to conclusions before you have thought them through. Let us take another example:

*A Sewell decided to increase the price of one of her products by 5% in December so that a bigger profit could be made at Christmas. In the January sales the unsold items were labelled '5% off'. Would you be paying the same, more, or less for the product in January compared to November?*

Let us work this one through:

Suppose the product is sold for £100 in November. The 5% increase in December would take this to £105 (£100 x 105%).

Now in January the decrease is 5% of the £105. £105 x 5% = £5.25. The product will therefore sell at £105 - £5.25 = £99.75.

So in January you would be paying less for the product than in November.

---

**WARNING!**

Some students will be quite used to percentages and so will be happy to go straight on at this point. If you are **not** one of these students, and are unused to percentage calculations, you should go back and read this chapter again. You should be quite happy with calculating percentages before you try the next section.

---

## CHAPTER 5
## Working with Numbers

**Calculating the cost price from the selling price**

It is quite usual for a company to decide on what profit they want to make on any particular product. Let us take another example:

> *J Milton reckons to make a 30% profit on each product he sells. The product sells for £1,560 each. What is the cost price to J Milton of each product?*

The danger here is that we simply take 30% of £1,560. This would be wrong because the 30% is on the cost price of the product and not the selling price. The method of calculating this is:

Cost price x 130% = £1,560 (the selling price)

You may be able to see that the £1,560 is 130% of the cost price. Therefore if you divide by 130 and multiply by 100 you will arrive at the cost price.

£1,560 ÷ 130 = £12. £12 x 100 = £1,200.

Don't worry if you don't follow the logic of the maths; you only need to remember the method.

We can check if our answer is right. If we increase the cost price by 30% we should get to £1,560.

£1,200 x 130% = £1,560

Let's take another example:

> *You decide to buy a new coat in the sale. The rack of coats is marked 'all coats on this rack reduced by 20%'. You choose a coat which now has a price of £120. What was the price of the coat before the reduction?*

This time we know that £120 is 80% of the original price, since 20% has been taken off the full price. If we follow the same method as before we get

£120 ÷ 80 = £1.50. £1.50 x 100 = £150

So the coat was originally £150.

We can check our answer again. 20% of £150 is £30. If we take £30 off £150 we get £120.

Working with Numbers

**How managers use percentages**

Managers like the use of percentages because they show results without the distraction of volume. A business may sell 100 items one year and 200 items the next. The amount of profit would presumably be different for each year, but by the use of percentages the profit can be calculated so that the effect of selling more items is taken away. Managers can then see how to run the business more efficiently apart from increasing sales.

Managers also like to see whether figures are favourable or unfavourable. This can be shown on the percentage change from period to period. If sales are higher then this is a favourable increase, but if costs are higher then it is an unfavourable increase.

**How precise should you be?**

Percentages are indicators of how well a business is doing. Being an indicator there is a limit on how exact we need the figures. Your calculator may well take your answers to several decimal places. To say that the net profit of a business has increased by 12.7356798% is no more useful (and more confusing) than saying it has increased by 12.7%. How precise to be is always a difficult question. The first rule is to follow company policy or past practice. If the previous set of results show two places of decimal (e.g. 12.73%, 15.26%, 9.25%) then you should follow this example. In the unlikely event that you are not told, two decimal places should be shown even if these are zeros (e.g. 16.00%).

Sometimes it is easier to show large figures much less precisely. Let us take an example of a string of figures:

274839, 276412, 277319, 271985, 274196.

It is not clear at a glance which figure is the largest or in what order they come. Unless you need to be very precise it is much easier to read if the figures are rounded to thousands. If we round the above figures to thousands we get:

275000, 276000, 277000, 272000, 274000.

The rules for rounding are given on the next page. When rounding to thousands the significant digit is the hundreds figure or the third figure from the right.

An extension of this is to **display** the numbers in thousands. This is very common where businesses have accounting figures in the millions or billions. It is a lot easier to see £1250 as representing one million, two hundred and fifty thousand that £1250000. The numbers are first rounded to thousands and then the last three zeros discarded. So in the previous example the numbers will be displayed as:

275, 276, 277, 272, 274.

71

You will need to state that the figures are displayed in thousands. This is usually done by a column heading of '£'000'. Remember though that if this column heading is used it is incorrect to display them in any other way. So if a column is headed £'000 and the figure below is 275000 the number represented is 275 million (and not 275 thousand).

If the figures are not in a column you can always state that the figures are displayed in thousands.

---

### ALERT!

You may need to 'round' the answer. This means bring it to the nearest number. I will use the term 'rounding digit'. This refers to the last number you want in your answer. So if you need to round to two decimal places the rounding digit will be the second decimal place.

When rounding numbers involving decimals, there are 2 rules to remember:

**Rule 1.** Determine what your rounding digit is and look to the right side of it. If that digit is 4, 3, 2 or 1, simply discard all digits to the right of it.

**Rule 2.** Determine what your rounding digit is and look to the right side of it. If that digit is 5, 6, 7, 8 or 9 add one to the rounding digit and discard all digits to the right of it.

Let us take a couple of examples.

Suppose we have 12.73498% and we want to round to two decimal places. The rounding digit is the second decimal digit, in this case, 3. The digit on the right of this is 4 so we simply discard all the digits on the right of the rounding digit – 12.73%.

Now let us suppose that we have 14.648432%. The rounding digit is 4. The digit on the right of this is 8 so we add 1 to the rounding digit and discard all the digits to the right of the rounding digit – 14.65%.

Be careful when the rounding digit is 9. Let us take an example 17.89741%. The rounding digit is 9 and the digit on the right of this is 7. We need to add 1 to the rounding digit. You must remember that this makes 10 and not just zero. The answer will be 17.90%. Since we do not normally show zeros at the end of a decimal (except when showing money e.g. £7.50) the answer will more correctly be 17.9%.

There are two points to remember. If company policy tells you to do this a different way then you must follow the company policy rules. The other point involves VAT. VAT has its own rules on rounding. The rounding rules for VAT are covered in the Indirect Tax book published by the same author.

# 2. Averages

Sometimes it is necessary to look at figures as an average. If we just have a mass of data it is sometimes difficult to see what it means, so an average will help us to simplify it. For example, suppose we have sales of a particular product over the last 5 days:

| | |
|---|---|
| Monday | 250 |
| Tuesday | 198 |
| Wednesday | 248 |
| Thursday | 250 |
| Friday | 269 |

Although we have the exact figures for each day, it is still a mixture of figures which isn't easy to use for planning. If we use an average we can reduce the five figures to one, which we can use for budgeting and planning.

There are three types of average; the mean, the mode and the median. The mode and the median are used more predominantly in statistics and data collection, but by far the most common is the **mean**. To calculate the mean you add up all the figures in your list and divide by the number of figures there are. In our example we calculate $250 + 198 + 248 + 250 + 269 = 1215$. Then we divide by 5 (the number of figures there are in the list).

$1215 \div 5 = 243$.

This is the same as saying that we would sell the same number of units if we sold 243 every day. You will note that 243 units were never sold on any one day, but we can plan our purchases a lot better if we can judge what we are likely to sell every day.

The next type of average is the **median**. Here we have to find the middle figure from our list. The first thing to do is put the figures in order from lowest to highest:

198, 248, 250, 250, 269.

We then choose the middle figure (the third figure along in this case); 250.

Sometimes you may not have an exact middle figure. This is the case if you have an even number of figures. Suppose our sales list included a Saturday figure; let's say 234. Now our ordered list would look like this

198, 234, 248, 250, 250, 269.

Now the middle is in between 248 and 250. If you need to find the median of this list you find the mean of the middle two figures. ($248 + 250 = 498$. Then $498 \div 2 = 249$.

73

The final type of average is the **mode**. This is simply the number which occurs most frequently. In our list all the figures occur once except 250 which occurs twice. Since the number 250 occurs the most number of times the mode is 250.

We can also use data in groups and find the mode. For example we wish to find the **modal** age of people who buy our goods. We may group them as follows:

Under 18

18 – 25

26 – 35

36 – 45

46 – 55

56 – 65

Over 65

Over a period of time we may use a **tally** (a mark for each item sold) against each age group of people who buy our goods. After a certain number of people we will add up our tally for each group.

| | |
|---|---|
| Under 18 | 79 items |
| 18 – 25 | 116 items |
| 26 – 35 | 87 items |
| 36 – 45 | 63 items |
| 46 – 55 | 27 items |
| 56 – 65 | 15 items |
| Over 65 | 5 items |

So in this example the modal group is 18 – 25 year olds.

## Chapter Summary

- Percentages are used to take away the influence of size, so that businesses can compare like with like, irrespective of how large a company is.

- Percentages are use to show how much an increase or decrease has been made in relation to previous years' figures

- Percentages are used to show an overall increase or decrease in cost irrespective of the volume.

- Care must be taken to ensure that the calculations show what you want them to show.

- Care must be taken when calculating a cost price from a selling price.

- Some figures need to be rounded. There are general rules for rounding.

- It is possible to round figures in thousands. These may also be displayed in thousands.

- It is sometimes useful to show average figures. There are three types of average: mean, median and mode. The mean is by far the most common.

# Chapter 5

# Practice Questions

**5.1**

Some Christmas cards have been reduced in January from £3.99 per pack to £2.65. What is the percentage reduction? Round your answer to one decimal place.

**5.2**

Your employees on the production line earn £420 per week. A pay rise of 5% has been announced. What will the new pay per week be?

**5.3**

A computer sells for £600. The store is having a sale where everything is reduced by 15%. What will the price of the computer be in the sale?

**5.4**

Car seat covers have a price tag of £45. The sign in the shop says everything has been reduced by 20%. What was the original price of the car seats?

**5.5**

'David's Deals' sells products at a profit of 15% on cost price. If a product sells at £217.35 what was the cost of the product to David?

**5.6**

The following results have been recorded for the last two years for W Auden. You are to complete the table by calculating the expenses and profits in relation to sales. You should round your answers to two decimal places.

| | 2013 £ | % | 2014 £ | % |
|---|---|---|---|---|
| Sales | 2,350,000 | 100 | 2,560,000 | 100 |
| Cost of Sales | 940,000 | | 1,075,200 | |
| Gross Profit | 1,410,000 | | 1,484,800 | |
| Wages and Salaries | 400,000 | | 486,000 | |
| General Office Costs | 200,000 | | 243,000 | |
| Total Overheads | 600,000 | | 729,000 | |
| Net Profit | 810,000 | | 755,800 | |

**5.7**

Show the figures for 2013 and 2014 from the table in task 4.6 in the table below.

| | 2013 £'000 | 2014 £'000 |
|---|---|---|
| Sales | | |
| Cost of Sales | | |
| Gross Profit | | |
| Wages and Salaries | | |
| General Office Costs | | |
| Total Overheads | | |
| Net Profit | | |

**5.8**

A company makes a product called Zhen. The factory workers have been timed making 15 of the products and the results are set out below:

1       36 minutes

2       35 minutes

3       31 minutes

4       41 minutes

5       30 minutes

6       37 minutes

7       29 minutes

8       32 minutes

9       36 minutes

10      33 minutes

11      32 minutes

12      35 minutes

13      37 minutes

14      30 minutes

15      36 minutes

You are to calculate the mean, the median and the mode averages for the time it takes to make a Zhen.

# Chapter 6

## Presenting Data

In this chapter we will look at presenting data in tables, graphs and charts. We will see that presenting data in an appropriate format makes interpreting figures much easier. We will look at the main types of graphs and charts and see how they are constructed. We will also see that the same data can be presented in different formats and that the format must be chosen with care to ensure the data is fit for purpose by the user.

Data is simply a collection of facts or figures. Data may be collected by many means. A stock check is a physical count of all items in stock. The result will be the data showing each item of stock and the quantity.

Data may also be collected from the records a business keeps. You may be asked to collect the data on sales revenue over the past 4 years. You could do this by looking into the records of the company and copying the data.

**Time series table**

The data is often put into a table to make it easier to read. For example

| DAWSON'S ENGINEERING Profit Statements | | | | |
|---|---|---|---|---|
| | **Year 1** £'000s | **Year 2** £'000 | **Year 3** £'000 | **Year 4** £'000 |
| Sales | 2,500 | 2,750 | 2,800 | 2,850 |
| Gross Profit | 1,250 | 1,300 | 1,330 | 1,380 |
| Net Profit | 225 | 270 | 260 | 280 |

When data is presented in time order (in this case years, but it could just as easily be months, weeks or days) it is called a **time series**. The time series table has several vital parts:

- A title. We need to know what the table is about.
- Equal time periods. It would be no use showing the annual figure in some columns and monthly figures in another.

- The time periods are clearly marked. It is customary to show time periods from left to right rather than top to bottom.
- The £'000s shows the figures are presented in thousands of pounds. So year 1's profit is actually £225,000. The reason for showing it like this is to make it easier to read. Figures are more difficult to read when lots of zeros are included. Of course, some rounding may be necessary, but accuracy to the nearest thousand pounds is often enough detail to show what is happening in the business.
- The details of what figures are presented are shown along the left hand side. Here it is sales, gross profit and net profit.
- The table is divided up by lines. This makes it absolutely clear which figure relates to which year and what each figure is about.

It is much easier to interpret the figures in a table like this than simply stating the data in a less formal way. For example we can see that sales and gross profit are going up each year, while net profit is going up in general, but with a downturn in year 3. The general movement upwards (or downwards) is called a **trend**. So from our table we can see that all the figures have an upward trend. The general movement over the years is upwards.

**Graphs and Charts**

While we can see from the table that the trend is upwards, it is not immediately apparent how much the figures are improving. This can be seen much more clearly if we show the figures in a graph or a chart.

**Line Graphs**

A line graph uses points connected by lines to show how something changes in value. The value of the sales is matched with the year and a point put on the graph where they meet. When all the points have been placed (plotted) the points are joined up with a line.

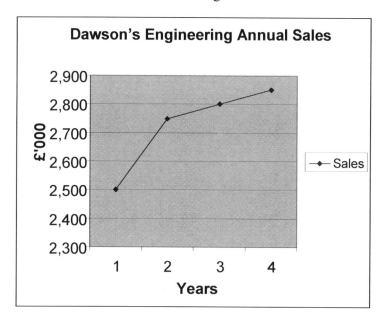

Let us look at the important features of a line graph.

- It must have a title. There is no point creating a graph if it doesn't tell others what it is about.
- It must tell us what the figures mean. Along the bottom (called the x axis) we should put the time scale (years, months, weeks, days) or it may even be the actual years (2012, 2013 etc)
- Along the left hand side (called the y axis) you must put what the figures are. In this case it is in thousands of pounds, but other cases could show units of production, number of employees, or whatever you are showing on the graph.
- You will notice that the figures don't go all the way to zero. Here they start at 2,300. If we had started the figures at zero there would be a great deal of space at the bottom of the graph with nothing in it. This may have shown us the level of the sales, but is not necessary here because we are only comparing one year to another and not each year to zero.
- A suitable scale should be chosen. In this case the figures are going up in 100s, but other graphs may fit better with figures going up in 50s, 1,000s or even ones. Whatever you choose it must go up by equal amounts.
- There should also be a key showing what the line represents. In this case the key is on the right hand side of the graph and shows that the line represents sales.

Presenting data as a graph makes it easy to see the trend and how this trend alters over time. The example above makes it easy to see that sales went up far more from year 1 to year 2 than in the other years, even though every year was upwards.

**Trends**

It is possible to draw a trend line on a line graph. The line is where the figures are used to show a general overall trend, usually by some sort of average. These trends can be calculated by different means and you will see later in your studies how to calculate some of them. For now we will just look at how a trend line fits on the actual results

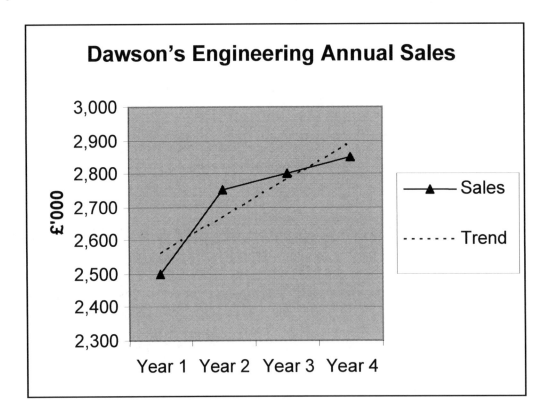

This trend line shows the sales are increasing but it takes away the yearly ups and downs and expresses it as an average increase. Trend lines are useful to see an overall trend and also for

forecasting. The trend line can be extended (extrapolated) for future years. This may give an idea of what might happen in the future if the general trend continues. You must use this with caution though as there are many factors which may cause the trend to change. At best the extrapolation of a trend line is no more than an educated guess.

You must be careful with graphs, as how you set out your graph may give you the wrong impression. Let us take the above graph and alter the scale.

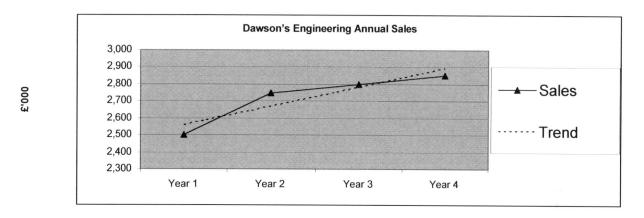

As you can see, the increase does not look so impressive in this graph, but if you check the information it is exactly the same. Choose the scale and format of your graph with care.

**Showing more than one set of data**

It is possible to show more than one set of data on a line graph. If we look back at the table of sales, gross profit and net profit, we can show all of these on one graph.

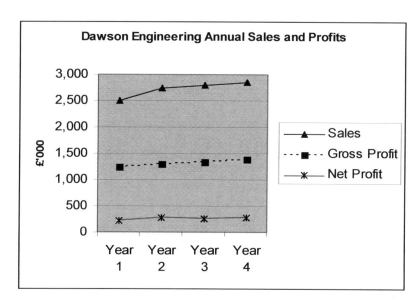

Here we can see all the data from the table in one graph. It is useful for comparing trends. In this graph we can see that in spite of rising sales, the net profit has remained nearly the same in comparison. A trend which goes neither up nor down is referred to as a flat (the line is flat and not going up or down).

Be careful when using more than one line. You should not show units and pounds on the same scale. The scale here is in thousands of pounds and you must keep to this.

**Bar charts**

The bar chart below represents the information in our table as a series of bars. The elements of the chart are the same as for a line graph in that there must be a title, axis labels and a key. The scale of the y axis will generally go down to zero. As there is just one set of data represented, it is known as a **simple bar chart**.

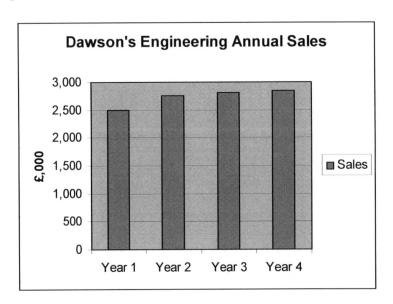

Just as with a line graph, how you set out your line graph will have an effect on the impression it gives. Take the following example:

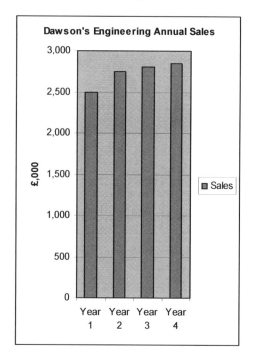

Here we have exactly the same information but shown in a different scale. It gives the impression at first sight that sales are much higher in the second chart, but actually they are the same.

As with the line graph we can show more than one set of data on one chart.

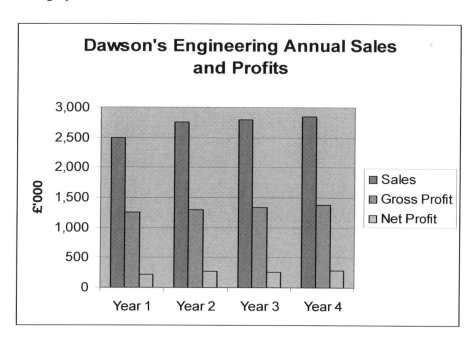

Here we can see Sales, Gross Profit, and Net Profit shown on the same chart. These types of charts are known as **compound bar charts**.

# CHAPTER 6
## Presenting Data

### Using bar charts to compare figures

Let us take another example of some data, this time showing sales in different branches of the company.

| VICKERS Sales by Branch | | | | |
|---|---|---|---|---|
| | Year 1 £'000s | Year 2 £'000 | Year 3 £'000 | Year 4 £'000 |
| Bristol Branch | 1,500 | 1,525 | 2,440 | 2,745 |
| Aberdeen Branch | 550 | 615 | 915 | 1,220 |
| Grimsby Branch | 450 | 610 | 610 | 1,830 |

We can use the bar chart to show the sales for each branch. This is known as a **component bar chart**. The sales for each branch are added to the top of the bar and the total height of the bar shows the sales for the whole company. Notice that all the elements of a chart are still present, including the title, axes labels and a key.

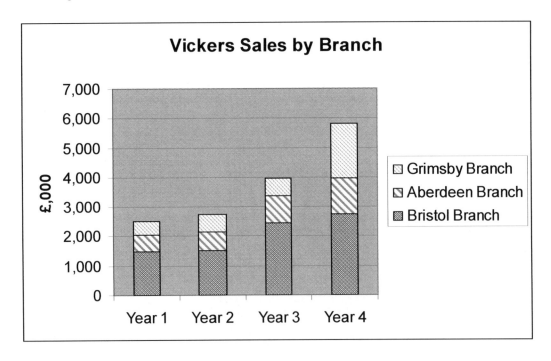

The same information shown on a line graph would look like this:

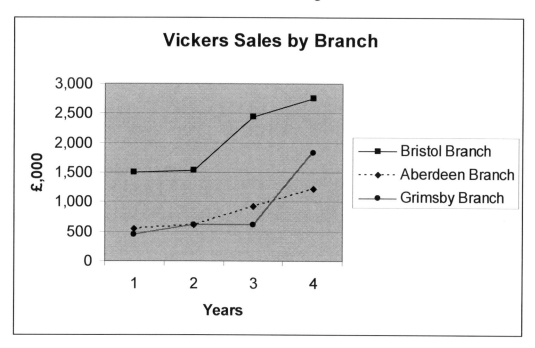

You must be careful how much data you put on one graph or chart. Had Vickers had 20 branches the graph and chart would have become very cluttered as 20 lines on a line graph or 20 parts of a bar chart would have been difficult to follow and would defeat the object of creating either of them. Remember that graphs and charts are created to make raw data easier to read and compare.

**Percentage component chart**

The same information can be shown as a percentage of the total for each branch. So for example we can see that in year 1 Bristol had 60% of the sales while Aberdeen had just over 20%. Grimsby had just under 20%.

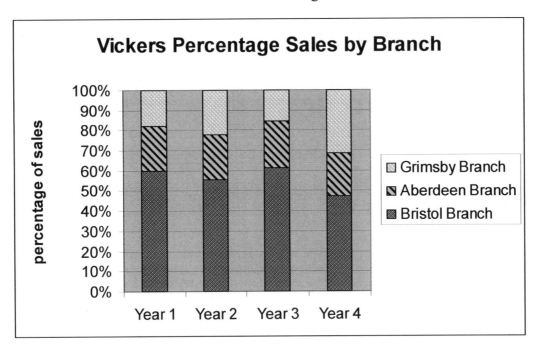

**Pie Charts**

A pie chart is a circular chart divided into segments. Each segment represents a proportion of the whole. Each circle (or 'pie') can only show one set of data at a time and the relationship of each part of the set to the total. In the following example the pie chart can only show the data for each year. In this case year 1 has been chosen although other pie charts could be constructed for the other years. The segments show how each branch has done in relation to the sales for the company as a whole.

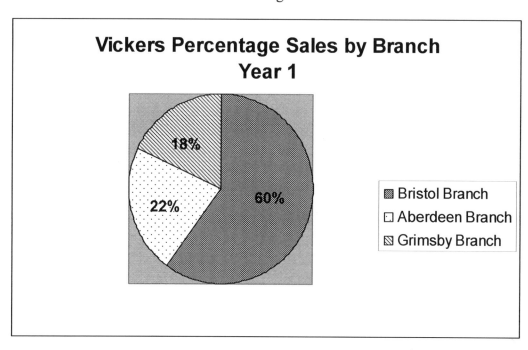

**Vickers Percentage Sales by Branch Year 1**

Pie charts can be constructed by hand with a protractor and drawing equipment.

You will first need to find out the percentage of sales each branch has in relation to the sales of the whole company. Taking the example for year 1 we can calculate that the sales for the whole company is £1,500,000 + £550,000 + £450,000 = £2,500,000. So for the Bristol Branch we calculate £1,500,000 ÷ £2,500,000 = 0.6. If we multiply the answer by 100 we get 60%. If, on the other hand, we multiply the answer by 360° (as there are 360° in a complete circle) then we get the number of degrees for the segment of the circle.
$0.6 \times 360° = 216°$

Let us do the same for the other two branches:

Aberdeen Branch          £550,000 ÷ £2,500,000 = 0.22

                         $0.22 \times 360° = 79.2°$

Grimsby Branch           £450,000 ÷ £2,500,000 = 0.18

                         $0.18 \times 360° = 64.8°$

Now, using your protractor, you can draw your own pie chart. Remember that the number of degrees is only of interest to the person constructing the chart. Your manager will have no interest in this at all and probably be annoyed at extra unnecessary data cluttering up what may be an important management document.

# CHAPTER 6
## Presenting Data

**Which format to choose**

In a real situation you may have to decide for yourself which kind of chart or graph to use. Bar charts are much favoured if the actual level of the data is required. Since the scale usually starts at zero then the height of each bar will be an indication as to the volume. In our examples the level of sales is indicated far better by the bar chart than the line graph.

However, if the information is required to show the trend then a line graph will show this far better than a bar chart, particularly if the trend is not particularly steep. It is easier for the eye to follow the path of a line than the path of the top of a bar. Pie charts are the most appropriate to show the relative proportion to the whole. In our example the pie chart shows more easily the relative contribution of each branch to the whole company.

Whichever graph, table or chart you are asked for, it is essential it is neatly presented. If you are constructing one manually, you must be sure that it is easy to read and that the data is appropriately labelled. Your manager will be less than pleased if he/she has gone into a top level meeting and cannot make head or tail of what is in front of him/her. If you have constructed one from a computer, you must make sure that the correct data has been selected and it has been presented in the way you (and your manager) would expect.

# Chapter Summary

- Data is a set of information collected in various ways.

- Data can be presented in various ways.

- Data is usually presented first in the form of a table.

- From the tables charts and graphs can be constructed.

- The main types charts and graph are:

    Line graphs
    Bar Charts
    Pie Charts.

- Bar Charts are either 'simple', 'compound' or 'component'.

- The degrees needed to construct a pie chart can be calculated manually and the chart can be constructed with a protractor and drawing equipment.

- Care must be taken when choosing which chart or graph to construct.

- Tables, charts and graphs can be constructed manually or by using a computer.

# **Practice Questions**

## **Chapter 6**

### **6.1**

The following financial data has been collected about Greens Garden Centres.

Dundee Branch

Sales   2011   £470,000
Sales   2012   £580,000
Sales   2013   £650,000
Sales   2014   £705,000

Wilmslow Branch

Sales   2011   £120,000
Sales   2012   £295,000
Sales   2013   £410,000
Sales   2014   £470,000

Slough Branch

Sales   2011   £410,000
Sales   2012   £350,000
Sales   2013   £295,000
Sales   2014   £350,000

Torquay Branch

Sales   2011   £175,000
Sales   2012   £235,000
Sales   2013   £295,000
Sales   2014   £300,000

You are to construct a suitable table to present this data.

### **6.2**

Using the table you constructed in task 5.1 construct a suitable compound bar chart showing the sales for all four branches over the four years

**6.3**

Using the table you constructed in task 5.1 construct a line graph to show the sales of all four branches over the four years. Comment on the trend for each branch.

**6.4**

Using the data in task 5.1 construct a pie chart for each year showing the relative sales for each branch.

This page is for your notes

# Chapter 7

## Methods of Communication

In this chapter we will see the need for effective communication.

We shall look at the various means of written communication.

We shall look at various formats of written communication.

We will see how businesses have their own unique identity through written communication.

We will see how to write an informal report.

To be effective in business you have to be a good communicator. As an Accounting Technician you may well have to communicate effectively with customers and suppliers as well as people in your own organisation.

First and foremost is the need to be polite. Being polite does not necessarily mean giving in to what the other person wants. Indeed, you may need to chase late payment from customers, which will need firmness as well as politeness. Being polite in itself will not always win your case, but by not being polite you will almost certainly not get your way or win your argument.

The greatest skill in effective communication is to see things from the other person's point of view. If you always say what **you** want and how **you** want to do things then you will make no progress in effective communication. While you should not let the other person control matters, you should always be receptive to their point of view and be ready to accept alternative ideas to achieve the goal you require. The only person you can be sure of changing is you, so if you can adapt what is required or how it is done to suit the other person, as long as it achieves the required goal, you are well on the way to promoting better relationships.

Most people tend to focus on what is wrong. Of course, you need to be clear on what the problem is, but you also need to be clear on what works well. So if you have a problem with a customer who is late paying his/her invoice, you need to say that, but you should also say how the problem can be resolved. Compare the following narratives

*"It is now over 2 months since we sent you Invoice No 12345. You haven't paid it yet and we need you to pay it immediately"*

*"We note from our records that Invoice No 12345 is still outstanding. Since it was sent over 2 months ago, it is now considerably overdue. We would appreciate settlement by return of post as per your usual method of payment."*

The second example is more likely to get a result than the first as you have stated the problem but avoided confrontation. There is also the solution to the problem. Of course if this doesn't get a result then you may have to be a little more firm, but this should be the kind of language you use in a first request letter.

You must be clear about what you mean and what your intention is. If you are not then other people can misinterpret what you mean (sometimes deliberately if it is to their advantage).

Don't make unconfirmed assumptions. For example, don't assume that someone hasn't paid their invoice because they hope to avoid paying it (even if you think this is what has happened). Assumptions aren't all bad as long as you state what they are. It is quite alright to say *"I assume the goods you bought arrived in good condition"*, and may lead to the reason for the request for payment.

Avoid conflict at all costs. Conflict rarely gets satisfactory results. State your case and accept the other person's point of view (even if you think it may be a lame excuse). *"I sent the cheque in the post last week"* should not be answered by *"well why haven't we got it?"* This is confrontational. You should accept their response but suggest how the problem can be resolved, in this case, either by tracing the cheque by its number or issuing a new one. If they are telling the truth then the problem can be resolved easily; if they're bluffing they won't be able to tell you the cheque number and will have to issue a new one anyway.

The way you respond also has a massive effect on the way you and your company are perceived. Being polite, efficient, firm, yet responsive will get you more customers than if you are not.

Business communication should never be 'chatty'. Usually business people don't have time for the niceties of unimportant information. While you should ensure that your communication covers all the required points and gives sufficient data, you shouldn't write two pages where two lines would do. Being succinct is an essential skill in business.

**The Note**

The simplest and most basic form of written communication in any organisation is the note. It is used as a quick and easy method of conveying messages between people, usually in the same or neighbouring offices or departments. Because it is quick and simple it is usually hand written.

A note should include

- The name of the person it is from
- The name of the person it is to
- The time and date the note was written
- A clearly stated message

An example note is shown below:

*To:*        *J Murray*

*Date:*      *24ᵗʰ November 2014*

*Time:*      *2.15pm*

*Mr Watts called from Asco Ltd. He wants to set a time for a meeting with you.*

*Please call back on 01752 627398 before 5.30pm*

*T Rose*

**Memorandum**

A memo or memorandum is a type of communication commonly used in businesses. Memos are sent to colleagues and co-workers. They are less formal than a letter, but more formal than a note. They do not require a salutation ('yours faithfully' or 'yours sincerely') or a closure statement as in business letters or even a signature or name at the bottom.

A memo is used as a written reminder or to convey a short proposal or some basic information. They are usually short and to the point. An example is given on the following page.

# Memorandum

**To:** M Hughes

**cc:** R Crockett

**From:** A Dawson

**Date:** 24th November 2014

**Re:** December Sales Forecast

---

Please can you supply me with your forecast for sales for next month by the end of the week.

I need the information for a meeting on 1st December.

Thank you

You will notice that the 'to' and 'from' are at the top along with a 'cc'. 'Cc' stands for 'carbon copy' and it tells you that a copy of the memo has gone to this person. ('Bcc' is also possible with electronic memos. It stands for 'blind carbon copy' whereby the recipient is not made aware that a copy has been sent to anyone else).

The sender's name is put at the top along with the date and a short title explaining the subject matter of the memo.

If other material such as documents or tables are enclosed these are listed at the end after you have put 'encl'. This ensures that the recipient is aware of the extra material and can see what should be there.

Memoranda (the plural of memorandum) can be hand written or word processed. Memoranda are often the most common form of written communication within a business and can be sent by email between departments or sites.

# CHAPTER 7
## Methods of Communication

**Fax**

Fax is the abbreviated form of facsimile. It is a system for the electronic transmission of images over telephone lines. Since it copies anything, both pictures and words can be sent by this means. Advertising material as well as letters and documents are sent between fax machines, and as long as you have the fax number (which will be similar to a telephone number) faxes can be sent anywhere in the world.

A fax header sheet is usually sent at the beginning of the fax to show

- Who it is to
- Who it is from
- The fax number and phone number
- The number of pages sent
- The date
- What the fax is about
- The names of anyone on copy

# Fax

| | | | |
|---|---|---|---|
| **To:** | L Lowe | **From:** | Dawson Supplies |
| **Fax:** | 01469 585444 | **Pages:** | 2 including this header |
| **Phone:** | 01469 585448 | **Date:** | 24th November 2014 |
| **Re:** | Copy Invoice | **CC:** | C Berry |

☐ **Urgent**      ☐ **For Review**  ☐ **Please Comment**      ☐ **Please Reply**      ☐ **Please Recycle**

# CHAPTER 7
## Methods of Communication

**The Email**

Email is short for 'electronic mail'. It is an electronic document (usually a message) sent from a computer to a person or group on the Internet or computers connected by a network. It can be used to send messages to a single person or a group of people. As with the memo, a 'cc' or 'bcc' can be used (see above).

When you open an email account you will be given (or you can choose) an email address. Email addresses come in two parts. The part before the @ sign is the local part, which is often the user name of the recipient. The part after the @ sign is the host name where the email will be sent before it is downloaded (collected). (@ is pronounced 'at'). The domain is often the email provider such as 'hotmail' for Microsoft or 'gmail' for Google. Alternatively it can be the name of the organisation that the recipient represents. The domain may also show the type of recipient (.com is a commercial organisation; .co is a company; although both these are used for individuals as there is no term for private addresses). Other examples are .org usually for non-profit making organisations and charities. Educational institutions use .edu or .ac while government uses .gov. The country of the domain is often added. Great Britain uses .uk while the United States uses .us and South Africa will use .za. A full email address could look like this

jsmith@sample.co.uk

Email addresses are usually all lower case letters (small letters as opposed to capital letters). If upper case letters (capital letters) are used then it may be sent to a different address.

Received emails are stored at the domain address until they are downloaded (often automatically when the recipient logs in). A list of emails received will be shown and they can be opened individually.

Email was originally designed to send simple text messages, but now technology has allowed colours and pictures to be sent in the message. Be careful with colours and pictures in emails as over-use can look unprofessional.

Documents can be attached to emails although most mail servers will restrict the size of files that can be attached.

On the next page is an example of an email ready to be typed.

You will see the 'to' box, where the recipient's email address should be typed and the 'cc' box if anyone else is to receive the email. Emails can be sent to more than one address by putting a comma between the addresses. All emails should have a 'subject'. This is a title describing the contents of the email and will be shown in the recipient's received list before it is opened. An attachment box will appear if there are documents attached showing the file name of whatever is being sent with the email. Email is usually free and is almost instantaneous.

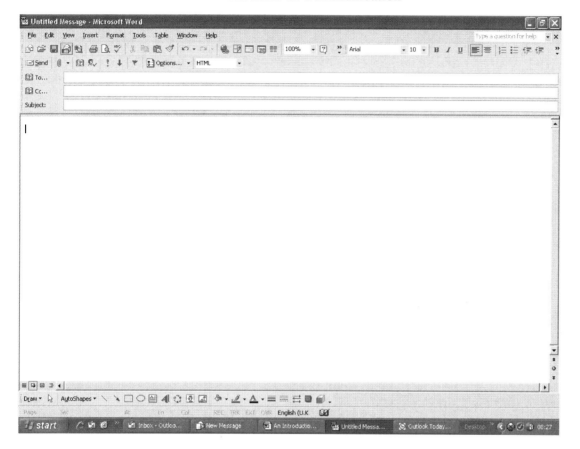

**WARNING!**

Opening an unsolicited email can cause unwanted downloads, especially of viruses, malware and adware. Some of these are programs designed to cause damage to the computer, while others cause advertising 'pop-ups' to appear while you are using other applications. Spyware are programs designed to monitor the users behaviour and can also collect personal and confidential information from the computer. These can also be downloaded from an email without the user's knowledge.

All computers should have an anti-virus program installed. While it will not guarantee the computer won't get infected, it will dramatically reduce the risk. However, even with an anti-virus program installed you should never open emails from unknown sources.

A growing problem with emails is *spam*. Spam is also known as "bulk e-mail" or "junk e-mail". It involves nearly identical messages sent to numerous recipients and often involves some kind of advertising. The real problem with spam is the sheer volume. As at April 2010 there were over 183 billion spam emails per day. The most popular spam topic is "pharmacy ads" which make up 81% of email spam messages. While most of the emails are harmless in themselves, the problem comes when the recipient's inbox becomes overloaded with spam. Some email inboxes may have over 100 spam items a day. Having to sort out the proper emails from the spam can be a time consuming (and annoying) task. Email addresses are collected from chat rooms and web sites and addresses may be sold to other 'spammers'. The amount of spam has been much reduced by better *filtering*. Filtering is where incoming emails are selected or rejected either by the sender's email address or by rejecting certain words in the title or content of the email. Filters are set up by the mail providers and can be adapted by the user if required.

Emails can be kept by the sender and the recipient on their computer almost indefinitely. This is useful if you wish to refer to the email in the future, but you may be subject to a limit by the provider or your organisation as these take up space in your computer's (or network's) memory. It is useful to check your old emails from time to time and delete unwanted items.

**Business Letters**

A business letter is a formal communication. To create the desired effect on the reader it is important to follow the following guidelines

- The letter should be in the correct format
- It should be short and to the point
- It should be relevant
- It should have no grammatical errors or spelling errors
- It should be polite (even if it's to complain or demand something)
- It should be neat and well presented.

The next page shows a typical business letter.

The key elements are

- Often the company name or logo (but not essential)
- Your address in the top right. (You could also include a telephone number and/or and email address here)
- The name (if possible) and address of who you are writing to goes below this on the left
- The position of the date is flexible but it usually goes below the addressee details
- The salutation at the beginning depends on whether you have the person's name. If you have then it should be 'Dear Mr Patel' or Dear Mrs O'Neil. If you don't know the marital status of a woman then you should put Ms. If you don't know the name of the person then you should put 'Dear Sir or Madam'.
- A heading is useful particularly if you are referring to something in the main text. This goes directly below the salutation

- If you are replying to a letter which has a reference number then you should repeat this number. Often this is just above the date.
- The content of your letter should be as short as possible, divided into short, clear paragraphs.
- End the letter with 'Yours sincerely' if you have named the recipient. Use 'Yours faithfully' if you've started with 'Dear Sir or Madam'.
- Sign your name and then print it directly below. If you are signing the letter in some capacity (e.g. Finance Administrator) then you should say so.
- If there are documents enclosed then say so by putting 'Encl'. You may want to state what they are.

---

DAWSON SUPPLIES                 **45 Scartho Street,
Immingham,
IM15 2BH**

The Purchasing Department
Patel Fabrics
132 Anglian Way,
Norwich,
NR3 6FG

1ˢᵗ December 2014

Dear Sir or Madam:

Invoice 123456

We note from our records that we have not yet received payment of invoice 123456 for £1650.00. Our terms are strictly 30 days and so this amount is due immediately.

I am enclosing a statement of account

Yours faithfully

Mr Alan Dawson
Finance Manager

Encl.   Statement of account

---

## CHAPTER 7
### Methods of Communication

A person in business may well receive many letters each day. If your letter is 6 sides of thick text then it may well end up in the bin. Letters should take seconds to read. As a result get straight to the point. Use straight forward language and don't use long words just for the sake of it. Don't repeat too much information which is on an enclosed document. The reader is quite capable of reading the document him/herself.

Spelling mistakes and bad grammar often give a bad impression of your company. If you are using a word processor then use the spell checker. Check the spelling yourself anyway as the spell check will not pick up all the errors (cf. 'their' and 'there').

Check the grammar. Some word processing packages will do this for you, but if not make sure you have written in complete sentences and check the punctuation. If you're not sure then you should get someone else to look at it.

Use the right tone of language. Avoid slang or colloquial language. It's better to say a company has gone into liquidation than the company has 'gone bust'. Avoid contractions ('it's', 'I'm') and don't use vague words such as 'nice' or 'get'. Don't use emotive words or subjective language ('rubbish' or 'great')

Always be polite even if you're complaining, and avoid too many long words and cliché phrases.

Make sure the letter is well presented. If it's hand written it should be neat and legible. Makes sure it's signed and dated and that you've spelt people's names correctly. Don't send a letter with coffee stains on it!

Many companies have a 'house style' letter. This is a uniform style of letter which will identify the company. House styles vary in complexity but will usually show the name, address and other details of the company and maybe the company's logo. All letters sent by the company will show this information in the same way.

House style letters may be printed stationery and extend to letters, faxes and memos as well as business cards and advertising material. Computers may store a template for letters and other stationery.

**The Report**

A report is a statement of the results of an investigation or of any matter on which definite information is required. Reports vary in their purpose, but all of them will require a formal structure and careful planning, presenting the material in a logical manner using clear and concise language. Later in the course you will be required to write an extended formal report. How to write a formal report is covered in the material for Internal Control and Accounting Systems of the AAT course. For now, however, we will look at how to write an informal report.

Before writing any report you should identify the reason you are writing the report and the type of presentation you will use. All reports attempt to communicate findings for one reason or another, whether to inform decision makers, change public opinion or maintain a record of development.

Whenever you write a report you must bear in mind why you are writing it and who you are writing for. All reports have an intended reader. Put yourself in their position. What do they need to know?

Reports are not essays. Reports are designed to give information which will be acted upon rather than read because the reader is simply interested in the topic. The report should be easy to read, clear and concise. You should use short sentences and avoid unnecessary jargon. Don't confuse conciseness with brevity. A report may be brief because it omits important information. A concise report, on the other hand, is short but still contains all the important information.

Formal reports should be written in the passive voice. 'I suggest …' is the active voice; 'It is suggested …' is the passive voice. Avoid naming names wherever possible; 'The Accounts Assistant' is better than 'Jane Smith'. This is less important in an informal report where it may be just one or two people who have requested the report and who will be looking at the report.

Avoid subjective language and pointless words. Words such as 'stunning', 'exciting', and 'fantastic' are all subjective in that they are only the opinion of the writer. Words and phrases such as 'basically', 'actually' and 'in the course of my investigations' all add nothing to the meaning of the sentence and only succeed in making the report less concise.

Avoid contractions. Use 'will not' and not 'won't'. Avoid slang. 'We ought to get a move on to make the rubbish figures a lot better', would be much better expressed 'Steps should be taken immediately to improve the poor figures'.

All reports have a series of sections. Often these sections are given headings. These sections may include the following:

An extended formal report will have a number of sections:

**The Beginning**

- Title
- Date
- Foreword
- Preface
- Acknowledgements
- Contents page
- Summary or Abstract
- Terms of reference
- Introduction

**The Middle**

- Methodology
- Findings
- Analysis

**The End**

- Conclusions
- Recommendations
- Appendices
- References
- Bibliography
- Glossary
- Index

Do not be concerned about the large number of sections that may be used; no report ever uses all of them. However, they are given here so that you can choose the most appropriate for your specific report.

The informal report will usually have just four of these sections:

- A title and date
- An introduction
- A findings or discussion section
- A conclusion and recommendations section.

**Title and date**

A report must always have a title. This may simply be what the report is about at the top of the page along with a 'to', a 'from', and a date. The 'to' is usually the person who requested the report and the 'from' will be the person who wrote the report. Don't forget to include their job titles.

Example

| | |
|---|---|
| To: | Nikoloz Gilauri, Finance Manager |
| From: | Maria Fekter, Accounts Assistant |
| Date: | 22nd January 2015. |

Report on Staff Training Requirements for the coming year.

## An introduction

This answers the questions, what, when, who and by when.

The 'what' is what the report is about.

The 'when' is when the report was requested.

The 'who' is who requested the report (usually the person to whom it is sent).

The 'by when' is the deadline for the report.

The introduction should be no more than 3 to 5 sentences.

## A findings or discussion section

This section will show the information that you have gathered or deal with the points requested. It is important to remember who the report is written for. Financial jargon, for example, may not be appropriate for the production manager.

Some managers will skim the report so it may not be read in a linear way. While it should be written with good grammar and spelling, the person reading the report may want to pick out the salient points quickly and easily. Subheadings could be used to pick out each point required (similar to the subheadings used in this book). Another way to format the report is to number the paragraphs. If you do so you should number all the paragraphs in all the sections. The paragraphs in section 1 (the introduction) should be numbered 1.1 and then 1.2 etc. Section 2 (the findings) will be numbered 2.1 and the 2.2 etc. Numbering paragraphs will only usually be necessary in longer reports.

If information has been gathered from other sources it is important to name the source. Your manager will want to know where you got your information.

The information should be set out in the most appropriate way. A new paragraph for each point or a subheading may be most appropriate in some cases, while a table or a chart might be better on another occasion. What you have to remember is who will be reading the report and what is the easiest way for that person to see what you have found.

**A conclusion and recommendations section.**

This section isn't always required. You shouldn't give personal opinions or recommendations unless you are requested to do so. If you do give a recommendation it should be based entirely on the findings in the report. You should never bring new information into this section.

The following suggestions will help you to produce an easily read report:

• Leave a space between each paragraph. Indent the paragraphs.

• Paragraphs should be short and concise.

• Headings should be clear - highlighted in bold or underlined.

• All diagrams and illustrations should be labelled and numbered.

---

**LEARNING POINT**

It is important to understand that reports vary in complexity and size. There is no one format which will cover all situations. The reports for this unit of the AAT course will be limited to one or, at most, two pages. The number of sections will vary according to what is asked by the question. You should choose appropriate sections to cover all the points required.

Whether to number the paragraphs depends largely on the length of the report. If a manager needs to refer to a particular paragraph it is easy to find it by using paragraph 2.7. However, on a one or two page report, numbering paragraphs is not usually required.

---

**ASSESSMENT ALERT**

You will need to know the format of each of the forms of communication explained above. Marks are awarded for the layout, spelling, grammar and appropriate use of language, as well as the content of any such communication.

## Chapter Summary

- Effective communication is an important part of any business

- There are several forms of written communication

  A note

  A memorandum (memo)

  A fax (facsimile)

  An email

  A letter

  A report

- Each of these has its own format and its own style of English

- Many of these have their own 'house style' which uniquely identifies the company

- Computer 'house styles' are kept as a template

- Reports have a formal structure.

- The structure is tailored to suit the complexity of the information and the needs of the user.

- Reports should be clear, concise and have an easy to read layout.

# **Practice Questions**

## **Chapter 7**

**7.1**

a)        On an email what is the meaning of Cc and Bcc?

b)        You need to send a copy of an invoice to your customer in the United States. What would be the quickest method of doing this?

**7.2**

You work at Dawson Supplies. Your manager comes to you saying that he has had a serious complaint from the buyer at T&T (Mr A Singh). Mr Singh has complained that although he ordered 20 rolls of fabric over a month ago he still hasn't received the goods. T&T is a valued customer and needs to be kept happy.

You check the records and find that the Purchase Order was received two days ago and delivery usually takes 1 week.

Your manager asks you to write a letter to Mr Singh at T&T. T&T's address is 154 Margaret St, Immingham, IM17 9RQ. Today's date is 1st May 2014. Show your response using the headed paper below.

DAWSON SUPPLIES                          **45 Scartho Street,**
                                                          **Immingham,**
                                                          **IM15 2BH**

**7.3**

You are the accounts assistant and you have been asked to prepare an informal report for the Managing Director, Richard Bray, on the importance of Health and Safety in the accounts office.

He has asked you to cover the following points:

The reasons for maintaining a Health and Safety policy.

A summary of legal requirements.

Health and Safety policy over and above the legal requirements.

The consequences of not complying with the legal requirements.

Today's date is Monday 21$^{st}$ January 2015 and Mr Bray requires the report by the end of the month.

**To:**

**From:**

**Date:**

**Report:**

**Task 7.3 (cont)**

**7.4**

You work in a bicycle store 'Two Wheels' and you have received the following delivery note from your supplier 'On Your Bike' which you have checked against the purchase order (on the following page).

## On Your Bike

127 St Martin's Street, Ipswich, IP1 6RQ

# DELIVERY NOTE

### NO. 26980

| To : | Two Wheels | Your Order Number : | 2398 |
|------|------------|---------------------|------|
| Address : | 37 South Street | Date Sent : | 1st June 2015 |
| | Salisbury | Per Invoice Number : | 136749 |
| | SP2 3EQ | Our Contact Person : | A Jamal |
| Attention : | V Symanski | Telephone : | 01722 437589 |

| Quantity Delivered | Description |
|--------------------|-------------|
| | |
| 2 | Cruiser bicycles (blue) |
| | |
| | |
| | |

**Goods received in good order**

| Name : | V Symanski | Signature : | *V Symanski* | Date : | *1/6/15* |
|--------|------------|-------------|--------------|--------|----------|

---

**Two Wheels**

37 South Street, Salisbury, SP2 3EQ

# PURCHASE ORDER

On Your Bike
127 St Martin's Street
Ipswich
IP1 6RQ

| **Invoice Address:** | 37 South Street | **Delivery Address:** | 37 South Street |
| --- | --- | --- | --- |
| | Salisbury | | Salisbury |
| | SP2 3EQ | | SP2 3EQ |

**Purchase Order No: 2398**

**Order Date 29th May 2015**

| Part Code | Qty | Description | Unit Price | Total Price |
| --- | --- | --- | --- | --- |
| | 2 | Cruiser bicycles (red) | £410.00 | £820.00 |
| | | | **Purchase Order Total:** | **£820.00** |

Authorised :   *V Symanski*          Date          *29/05/2015*

All orders are raised subject to our Terms and Conditions of trade. A full copy is available on request.
E&OE. All prices exclude VAT.

---

Use the following headed paper to write a letter to the supplier, explaining what is wrong with the delivery. Use your own name and the title Accounts Assistant. Today's date is 2nd June 2015

TWO WHEELS

**37 South Street,**
**Salisbury,**
**SP2 3EQ**

**7.5**

Send a memo to the stores manager to explain what has happened with the bikes from task 6.4. The stores manager is A Khan. Put the owner (V Symanski) on copy.

# Memorandum

**To:**

**cc:**

**From:**

**Date:**

**Re:**

---

**7.6**

In the following situations, which form of communication would be best?

a) You have received an email from a customer complaining that the wrong goods have been delivered.

b) While you are at lunch, the branch manager has come to your office for a sales invoice which a customer has queried. Your colleague tells you that the branch manager wants a copy of the invoice as soon as you return. The branch manager says he will be in the offices the other side of town.

c) The office manager asks you to circulate to all staff that the annual staff social evening will take place on 24th July.

d) A letter has been received from a customer complaining that the goods he has received are of poor quality.

e) While your colleague is away from the desk, a customer phones asking to speak to her. You say you will pass on the message. However, you are due to go to lunch in five minutes.

This page is for your notes

# Chapter 8

## Organising your own Work

In this chapter we will see the difference between 'effective' and 'efficient'.

We shall look at 'aims' and 'objectives'.

We shall see that managers must comply with the job description when allocating work.

We shall look at the difference between 'urgent' and 'important' and see why this is important in planning the day's work.

We will see how to prioritise work.

We will look at the planning aids which help us to plan and prioritise tasks in the workplace.

In the workplace you must be both efficient and effective. One without the other is not sufficient. Let us look at each in turn.

Being **effective** is about doing the right things, while being **efficient** is about doing things in the right manner. Let us suppose that two members of staff are scheduling the tasks they need to do throughout the day.

The first employee may look at the tasks and decide to start the first one. After 15 minutes he/she may tire of that particular task and go on to another one. The third task is started half an hour later after deciding that the second one can't be completed until the afternoon. The third task is a difficult one and the employee has a few attempts at it before getting it right in the end. The employee goes back to the first task and decides it needs some further information so he/she goes to the relevant manager to get it. The fourth task now takes his/her fancy and so this is started but then they find that it can't be completed until a colleague returns from a business trip later in the day. Eventually all the tasks are completed to the manager's satisfaction but not until the end of the second day. This employee can be considered effective (since all the tasks have been completed) but not efficient (since it has taken far longer to complete than was expected).

The second employee starts by looking at the tasks. He/she makes a list of what is to be done. The list is printed on the computer and estimated times are added. A second list of what information is required and from whom is made up. The lists are printed off and he/she goes and laminates them so they look professional on his/her desk. The lists are then placed neatly in a folder and the folder is stored neatly in the drawer so that it is easily accessible when it is required. It takes the employee only one hour to prepare the lists. This employee can be considered efficient (since the lists have been produced in only one hour) but not effective (since none of the task which are required have been done).

Working in an office is about balancing effectiveness with efficiency. It is about getting the job done with the minimum of wasted effort and resources.

All parts of a business have aims and objectives. Aims and objectives are always linked but are quite distinct. **Aims** are the changes you hope to achieve as a result of your work. **Objectives** are the activities you undertake to achieve these changes.

The aim of a business may be to make a profit of £50,000. The objective may then be to make sales of £200,000. In the office, your aim may be to complete eight tasks by the end of the day. You objectives may be to complete each task to a specific time scale.

The most effective business objectives meet the following criteria:

**S – Specific** – objectives are aimed at what the business does. The objective is concrete and well defined. For example, a car show room may have the objective of selling 40 new cars during October, an objective specific to that business.

**M - Measurable** – the business can put a value to the objective, e.g. £250,000 in sales in the next half year. It need not be a monetary measurement. Measurement is the standard used for comparison.

**A – Achievable** – Objectives still need to stretch you, but not so far that you become frustrated and lose motivation. Consideration of the timeframe and resources will be needed.

**R - Realistic** – the objective should be challenging, but it should also be able to be achieved by the resources available. To be realistic you must have the required resources, such as, people, money, skills, equipment and knowledge.

**T- Time specific** – they have a time limit of when the objective should be achieved, e.g. by the end of the year. Deadlines create the necessary focus, help set priorities and prompts action.

If you are to organise your own work you will need to set objectives and the best way of doing this is the S.M.A.R.T. way.

Organising your own Work

## Job Description

A job description outlines an employee's day to day tasks and also their responsibilities. When employing staff the employer should ensure that the employee is suitably knowledgeable and experienced to carry out the tasks detailed in the job description. Job descriptions are based on job analysis, so that there is an understanding of the competencies and skills required to accomplish the needed tasks.

Managers should therefore not ask employees to carry out tasks not covered in the job description. Employees should not be expected to (and should not attempt to) carry out tasks for which they are not skilled or experienced. Doing so could lead to mistakes which could harm the effectiveness and efficiency or the business.

## Planning and prioritising

It is important to identify what tasks need to be done and what type of tasks they are.

**Routine** tasks are those carried out on a regular basis. Routine tasks may include answering emails, delivering the post, photocopying or raising invoices. Routine tasks can be easily planned for, since they are those you do every day or every week. However, routine tasks must be carried out efficiently to maintain the smooth running of the business.

**Non-routine** task are those which are unexpected. They may include special assignments or projects. They may be of great importance, such as covering for an absent member of staff, or they may be mundane, such as calling out the repair person for the photocopier. Either way, non-routine tasks can sometimes cause problems, as they may hold up the routine tasks.

**Urgent** tasks are those which must be carried out by a specific imminent deadline. You may be asked to provide some information for a customer who is waiting on the phone, or the manager may require you to print out a document which he needs to take with him to the meeting in half an hour.

You should not confuse urgent with **important**. Important tasks are those which strongly affect the course of events. It is important that staff are paid their wages on time, but if payday is three weeks off it is not yet urgent.

**Prioritising** tasks is an essential skill. You can't do all the tasks you are required to do at the same time, so you will have to make a decision on what order you will do the tasks. What tasks you will do and in what order will depend on urgency, importance, and, of course, time.

Tasks can be grouped into four categories:

1. Urgent and important.
2. Urgent but not important.
3. Not urgent but important.
4. Neither urgent nor important.

As a general rule, you will carry out the tasks in the order shown above. You will find exceptions to the order, but in most cases you will follow them in the order shown.

You must be sure what is important and what is urgent so the first thing you must do when prioritising your work is to group them in the four categories. If your tasks are non-routine, you may not be sure what is important and what is urgent. Get feedback from others about what they consider the highest priorities. What they consider to be urgent or important may not coincide with your own personal view. It can be interesting to hear another person's perspective.

Always saying 'yes' to requests for last minute jobs can get you into trouble at times. It can cause you to be overworked, stressed and frustrated. Saying 'no' on the other hand can lead to confrontations. You must practice ways of saying 'no' without saying no.

"I'm happy to help you with that but firstly I need to prioritise this piece of work. Could you come back to me later?", is a lot more considerate than "I'm busy with this, so I can't", or "I' haven't got time".

Managing your time at work correctly means higher quality work, not higher quantity. Spending more time on a project doesn't necessarily achieve more. Staying late in the office may make you less productive through tiredness or frustration. Many people work through their lunch break, but this can be counter-productive. A break is an opportunity to relax and think of other things apart from work. You'll come back in the afternoon refreshed and more effective.

**Planning Aids**

Trying to complete the tasks of the day most efficiently can't really be done by simply keeping them in your head. You become more focused if you write down the tasks and prioritise them.

The simplest planning aid is the **'Post-it' note**. A Post-it note (or Sticky Note) is a piece of stationery with a strip of re-usable adhesive on the back, designed for temporarily attaching notes to documents and other surfaces. Sticking a 'Post-it' note in a prominent place will remind you important tasks you have to do, particularly the non-routine tasks.

Post-it notes

A more useful aid is a **'To Do' list.** Making a list of the day's tasks is very common both at home and at work. A simple shopping list can be considered as a 'to do' list. They can be written or compiled on the computer (see below). The tasks can then be ticked off as

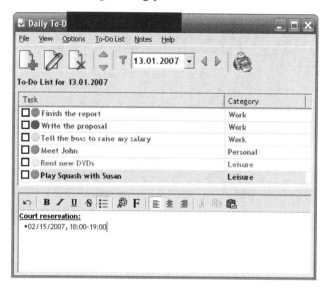

they are completed. A 'to do' list is a prioritised list of all the tasks you need to carry out, with the most important tasks at the top and the least important at the bottom.

There should be three steps to compiling a 'to do' list:

1. Write down all the tasks you need to complete.
2. Allocate a priority to each task. You may want to use the priority numbers shown on p108.
   If you have too many high priority tasks you may have to go through the list again and demote some that aren't quite so important.
3. Rewrite the list in priority order.

'To do' lists are also available for mobile phones, with alerts for when a task should be started or finished.

'To do' lists can be subdivided to show the priorities. So your list could have a subheading of 'Urgent Tasks' and then a subheading for 'Non-Urgent Tasks'. Items which are not ticked off by the end of the day will be carried forward to the next day.

'To do' lists are useful when there are a relatively small number of tasks. They can become cumbersome when there are too many items on them.

**A diary** may be kept. These are very useful in a number of ways. If kept correctly, they will not only act as a 'to-do' list, but they will also ensure events don't clash. Online diaries are widely available which have alerts for when a task should start, when you should prepare for starting a task and when the task should be complete. Applications are available for mobile phones.

# CHAPTER 8
## Organising your own Work

There are more complex planning tools for more complex activities. They are used mainly for projects which take many days of planning. They have a generic term of **'planning schedules'**. The most common planning schedule tool is a Gantt chart. How to set up a Gantt chart is beyond the scope of this book, but basically it lists all the tasks required for a project, when it is possible to start them and how long it is likely to take. An example is given below.

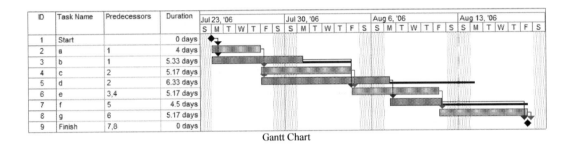

Gantt Chart

Here we see that (for example) task (c) cannot be started until the Friday and will take just over 5 days.

---

**ASSESSMENT ALERT**

You will not need to know how to set up a planning schedule but you may be required to interpret one so you know how to plan your own daily schedule. You may also have to set your own weekly schedule, so ensure you know what the task is. You can't schedule the Friday meeting for Tuesday but you may be able to start to compile the monthly figures required by Friday evening on Thursday afternoon.

---

Once you have identified the tasks required and set them in your planning schedule, you will need an **action plan**. The action plan can take any form, but it will do the following:

- Define each task in detail
- State who is responsible for each activity
- Establish a target completion date.

Some action plans will have more details such as the budgeted cost of each activity or there will be space to show the progress (such as meeting arranged date).

In its simplest form it will show the what, how, and when of each task. An example is given below:

| Proposed Action | The tasks involved | Who is responsible | Completion date |
|---|---|---|---|
| Purchase construction materials | Seek suitable suppliers | Purchase Manager | End of March 2015 |
| | Ensure funds are available | Finance Manager | April 14th 2015 |
| | Ensure delivery time. | Logistics Manager | April 21st 2015 |
| Construct the building | Ensure suitable staff are available | HR Manager | End of April 2015 |
| | Ensure ground is cleared | Site Manager | May 1st 2015 |
| | Arrange construction equipment to be delivered | Site Manager | May 1st 2015 |

The action plan will be complete when all the tasks in the planning schedule have been included.

The best laid plans don't always go as you expected them. A colleague may be off sick, your emails may not work because of a fault or the photocopier may not be working. You should then know how to re-prioritise your work. You will have to reassess your urgent and important tasks. You may have to re-write your 'to do' list.

However, you should always **communicate** problems and changes to priorities as the problem may impact on the work of others. You should negotiate with colleagues and managers as to the best way to overcome the problem. Managers will also want to see that the work is being completed without any hitches.

Whether there are problems or not, you should always **monitor** your work. At least once each day you should check that the work you have scheduled is going according to plan. Priorities may change or tasks may take longer than anticipated. In these cases a change in the planned priorities may be required. You may have to delegate some work; you may have to seek help from a higher authority, or you may have to carry forward work to the next day.

## Chapter Summary

- Being effective is about doing the right things, while being efficient is about doing things in the right manner.

- Aims are the achievements you strive for. Objectives are the activities you undertake to achieve these aims.

- The most effective business objectives meet the S.M.A.R.T. criteria.

- Managers should not allocate tasks to employees outside their job description.

- Some tasks are planned (routine) but others are not planned (non-routine).

- Tasks should be prioritised according to whether they are urgent or important.

- Planning Aids include:

  Post it notes

  To do lists

  Diaries

  Planning schedules

  Action Plans

- Employees should monitor their work priorities regularly and should be able to deal with changed priorities.

- Any problems should be communicated to other colleagues and managers.

# **Practice Questions**

## **Chapter 8**

**8.1**

Which of the following statements best describes effectiveness in the workplace?

a) The degree to which objectives are achieved.

b) The comparison of what is actually produced with what can be achieved.

c) Having the right resources to get the job done.

d) Following the company policy.

**8.2**

Which of the following statements best describes efficiency in the workplace?

a) The degree to which objectives are achieved.

b) The comparison of what is actually produced with what can be achieved.

c) Having the right resources to get the job done.

d) Following the company policy.

**8.3**

Being efficient and effective in the workplace means which of the following? Choose only the most suitable answer.

a) Doing things in the same way as they have been done previously

b) Asking your boss how to do the job.

c) Getting the job done with the minimum of wasted effort and resources.

d) Following the company policy.

# CHAPTER 8
## Organising your own Work

**8.4**

Below is a business's aim and its objectives. Say which is the most likely aim and then say which are the relevant objectives to that aim.

a)  Reduce the wage bill by £5,000 over the next two years.

b)  Maximise profits.

c)  Increase the sales of last year by 5% by December.

d)  Negotiate a new contract with the office cleaning company for another year.

e)  Negotiate a 2% discount on raw materials for the coming year.

**8.5**

Identify the most effective (S.M.A.R.T.) business objectives for a company's aim of increasing brand awareness.

a)  Negotiate an advertising campaign with ITV North for 20 advertisements a week for the next 12 weeks.

b)  Promote the brand on popular web sites.

c)  Design a new brand label for the brand by the end of the month.

d)  Rent 20 billboard spaces by the end of the quarter.

e)  Invest in a range of corporate gifts to be available by June.

# CHAPTER 8
## Organising your own Work

**8.6**

It is Monday and you are to identify the following tasks in the workplace as:

1. Urgent and important.
2. Urgent but not important.
3. Not urgent but important.
4. Neither urgent nor important.


a) Open the post and deliver it appropriately.

b) Report a fault with the computer database.

c) Collate the sales figures from all branches for next week's board meeting.

d) Water the plants in reception.

e) Make a collection for one of your colleagues who is getting married next month.

f) Check your 'to do' list.

g) Buy more coffee for the staff kitchen as there is none left.

h) Take the old sales files from the office and archive them in the archive store.

i) Print out the customer activity reports for a sales team meeting on Friday.

j) Chase up a customer whose account is 2 months overdue.


**8.7**

What planning aids are you likely to see on the accounts assistant's desk to help plan the daily work?

a) A Gantt chart

b) A diary

c) Post-it notes

d) An action plan

e) A to do list

This page is for your notes

# Chapter 9

## Team Working

In this chapter we will see the advantages and disadvantages of working in a team.

We shall look at the roles within a team.

We shall see what makes a good team member.

We shall look at what makes an effective team.

We will look at what causes conflict within a team and how conflicts can be resolved.

We will see how a grievance can be applied.

Working as a team implies a group of people working together, but this can be said about any workplace. Team working is a little more specific and is when a group of people work together, share the load of the given task and distribute work among themselves while keeping in mind the common goal.

A team consists of more than one person, each of whom has different responsibilities, but with one goal in mind.

**Advantages of teamwork**

If the team has been chosen carefully, there can be a good range of abilities, fields of expertise and personality types. So for every situation there should be at least one person who can deal with it. The benefits can be categorised as:

- **Creativity**

    We all have different skills, knowledge and personal attributes. By utilising all of these different aspects in a team, more ideas can be generated. As more ideas are generated, more creative solutions are generated, leading to better results.

- **Satisfaction**

Members of a team are working towards a common goal. As the members interact, more energy and enthusiasm is created. This energy and enthusiasm results in positive motivation and leads to even more success.

- **Skills**

No one has all the skills to do everything, but some may excel at certain tasks. Some may be good at one type of task while another may be good at a different type of task. Using people in a team will extent the range of skills available for the task.

- **Speed**

If one person were to be allocated a project, they would only be able to do one task after another. However, with a team many tasks can be undertaken at the same time.

- **Sounding board**

An individual may have a range of possible options. Figuring out what is best may take some time, and probably some false starts, if it is left up to an individual. In a team, the members can ask for other members' opinions and so quickly decide which are most likely to achieve the desired goal.

- **Support**

You should never underestimate the significance of support. People will go to extreme lengths if they know they can rely on the support of others. Support may take the form of advice, moral support or assisting with difficult tasks.

## Disadvantages of teamwork

Many managers see teamwork as a positive way of working. However, it does have its disadvantages.

- **Unequal participation**

There can be a tendency for some team members to sit back and let the others do all the work. This can cause resentment, especially if the business recognises the efforts of the team rather than the individual members.

- **Non Team Players**

Some people simply don't function well in a team. While they may be excellent workers in the right environment, they may not perform well when they have to fit into a team.

- **Limiting creativity**

  Members of a team may be so focused on working for the overall good of the team that they put their own innovative ideas to one side in order to fit into the team concept.

- **Longer process**

  There are a variety of processes which a team will need to go through which an individual will not. There is the team selection, organisation of the tasks, reviews of what has already been completed and deciding on what should happen next. In addition a team may tie up valuable resources such as money, manpower and equipment.

- **Inherent conflict**

  In any group of people there will be contrasting personal styles. Sometimes this may lead to conflict. Some members may have difficulty accepting ideas that differ from their own. Pressure from other members may result in someone going against their better judgement.

## Team roles

People adopt different roles in a team. These roles are not always constant. One person may adopt several roles, or they may change roles depending on the needs of the team. A good team may consist of:

- **The Leader**

  All teams need a leader. They may be natural leaders, appointed by the team or appointed by the company. They will direct the sequence of tasks required to achieve the team's goal. They will be good at controlling people and coordinating resources. They have determination to overcome obstacles. A good leader should recognise the skills of the individual and know how best to use these skills. They must be careful not to become domineering and impatient when it seems there is lack of progress.

- **The ideas person**

  This person will suggest new ideas to solve group problems or new ways to organise the task. They provide original suggestions. They are more concerned with the bigger picture than with the detail. They may get bored after the initial plans are implemented.

- **The implementer**

  These are people who get thing done. They turn the team's ideas into practical actions. They usually work systematically and efficiently and are well organised. They may be inflexible and resistant to change.

- **The encourager**

These are people who provide support and make sure that the people within the team are working efficiently and effectively. They may be the negotiators within the team. They have a tendency to be indecisive.

- **The specialist**

These are people with specialist knowledge that is needed to get the job done. They are the experts in certain areas. This may limit their contribution to the team and be preoccupied with technicalities at the expense of the bigger picture.

**What makes a good team member?**

Obviously, teams must have members who have the right technical abilities. But a team is not simply about pooling technical abilities. A good team will produce more than the sum of its parts. In other words a good team will produce a better result than each of its individual members could produce alone. In addition to technical skills a good team member should the following qualities:

- **Reliability**

A reliable team member gets the work done and does his/her fair share of the work. They will follow through assignments and meet commitments. You should be able to rely on a good performance all the time, not just some of the time.

- **Good communicator**

A team member should express their ideas and thoughts positively, confidently and respectfully.

- **Listener**

Teams need people who can consider ideas and points of view from other people without arguing every point. They should also listen to and consider criticism of themselves without reacting defensively.

- **Active participant**

Good team members ask themselves what they can do for the good of the team. They come to meeting prepared to speak up with ideas and suggestions.

- **Openness and willingness to share**

  Team members should be willing to share their information, knowledge and experience. They should keep other team members informed, not only at meetings, but also informally.

- **Cooperation**

  Effective team members act with others to get things done. They should work with other team members to solve problems and respond positively to requests for help.

- **Flexibility**

  Good team members should be able to accept and adapt to changing situations. They should be prepared to try something new or take a new direction. They should consider different points of view and compromise when needed.

- **Commitment**

  Team members should be committed to the team. They should make a good effort all the time and they will expect other team members to do the same.

- **Problem solver**

  A team member should get problems out in the open for discussion. They should plan ways of solving problems and not dwell on the problem itself. They should not apportion blame when a problem arises, but they should look on the problem as a challenge and something which needs to be overcome.

- **Respectful and supportive**

  Team members should treat others with courtesy and respect. They should show understanding of others and provide help and support. They should not place conditions on when they will help or when they choose to listen.

**What makes an effective team?**

A team can be a group of people who work together on a regular basis or have been chosen for a specific project. Whatever the purpose of the team it will only be effective if:

- It has a range of individuals who contribute in different ways.

- There are clear goals which everyone understands.

- Everyone understands the tasks they have to do.

- It has a coordinator or leader who is accepted by everyone. The leader may change for different tasks.

- The members feel free to criticise in a constructive manner.

- The team is comfortable with disagreement and can overcome differences.

- Members listen to each other and everyone's ideas are heard.

- There is a supportive atmosphere.

- The group reviews and improves performance in the light of past successes and failures.

Before effective team working can be established, it is important to remember that every one person is unique and, as a result, have differing needs, emotions and objectives. It is impossible to build up a relationship with someone unless you have a good understanding of what these things are and to accept these even if they differ from your own.

The most effective way of coming to understand your colleague is to listen to what they have to say carefully. This can lead to mutual respect and understanding being established and is a key factor in developing a good working relationship. If the relationship is a productive one, people will have no difficulty in being open and honest about their feelings.

Each individual should be encouraged to make their own contribution to discussions. It is even healthy to encourage debate on key topics so that each person has the opportunity to voice their opinion. By making people feel that their view is important and respected by others, more effective relationships can be established.

**Conflicts within a Team**

It is inevitable that there will be conflict within a team at some point. A team is made up of a group of individuals, all who have differing personal goals and opinions, so it is not unexpected for some of these goals and opinions to clash.

The most common causes of conflict within a team are:

1. **Interdependence**

   This is when a person relies on another's cooperation or input in order for them to get their own job done. For example, a salesperson is constantly late with the monthly sales figures, which causes the accountant to be late with their report.

2. **Difference in styles**

People differ in the way they get their job done. For example one person may try to get their work done as quickly as possible, while another may be more concerned that everyone has a say in how the job gets done.

3. **Personality Conflicts**

This is simply when people just don't get on together. One person may see another as loud and brash, whereas the other sees the first as retiring, non-cooperative and relying on others to get the job done.

4. **Conflict of Interest**

An individual may try to fight for their own personal goals and lose sight of the team's goals.

5. **Unclear Definition of Responsibility**

Many conflicts occur because their areas of responsibility have not been defined clearly enough. One person may see someone else as doing the job they have responsibility for, or one person may see another as not covering all the jobs they are supposed to do.

6. **Limited Resources**

Many conflicts occur because there is competition for the use of resources. For example, one person may be using the photocopier to print a 100 page report when another needs to print off a document for a meeting in half an hour.

Communication is both the cause and the remedy of conflict. If the aims and (particularly) the objectives of the team are too vague, conflict will occur. It is important, therefore, that aims and objectives are clearly defined and agreed at a very early stage.

**Resolving Conflict**

The best resolutions to conflict are those which come from the individuals themselves. The first approach in any conflict should be with the person involved. Talking to the person face to face is a lot better than emails or memos if at all possible. If you do this you should keep certain points in mind:

- **Be Calm**

  Conflict usually arouses strong emotions, but in an enraged state you are unlikely to achieve any compromise or even able to keep rational.

CHAPTER 9
Team Working

- **Always show respect**

Attack the argument and not the person. You are unlikely to reach any kind of resolution if you dishonour the person.

- **Be magnanimous**

In truth, many conflicts are over matters with little substance and often it is only pride or status which is at stake. Consider conceding the point. If you concede with good grace you may even make your opponent look small minded.

- **Acknowledge the other person's point of view**

It is not usually the facts alone which cause conflict, but how the facts are seen by the other person. Try to see things from another perspective. If you can't, ask them to explain their point of view. Above all, listen to what the other person has to say.

- **Beware of displacement**

This is where the source of a conflict is not always what it seems to be. For example, an argument about use of the photocopier could in fact be an argument about lack of recognition for the hard work already completed by the team member.

- **Use words wisely**

Avoid statements which can make the situation worse. Instead of criticising a colleague for a 'mistake', perhaps you could invite the colleague to discus a 'learning opportunity'. Instead of saying "You should do it this way", say "You might want to consider this option". Once spoken, words can never be taken back, so consider what you have to say before you say it. Particularly in situations of stress, count to three before you answer.

- **Compromise**

You may consider doing things partly your way and partly the other person's way. Try to make concessions. Don't be dogmatic in thinking that your way is the only solution. In many cases there is a third way which is neither your nor your colleague's way.

- **Seek mediation**

If the individual approach does not work it may be necessary to call in a third party. The third party may be the line manager or the office manager or the other members of the team. They will be asked for their opinion on the dispute and may be asked to suggest a solution.

You won't resolve a conflict by staying quiet. Ignoring the problem and hoping it will go away will not help the situation. Even worse will be to talk to other colleagues behind the other person's back in the hope of gaining their support. Of course, it may be worthwhile observing other colleagues to see if they have similar issues or even asking if they have any problems with the person concerned, but you must avoid gossip or being seen to try to get others on your side. You must not only be objective, but you must also be seen to be objective.

**Disciplinary and Grievance Procedures**

If the working relationship problem is of a very serious nature (such as bullying or harassment) the matter should be taken up with a higher authority immediately.

All employers must have a disciplinary procedures document and a grievance procedures document. Employers use disciplinary procedures to tell employees that their performance or conduct isn't up to the expected standard and to encourage improvement. Grievances are concerns, problems or complaints that employees raise with their employer.

Grievances can include:

- terms of employment
- pay and working conditions
- disagreements with co-workers
- discrimination
- not getting statutory employment rights

A grievance procedures document will normally suggest the employee tries to resolve the problem informally in the first instance, by speaking to the individual concerned or by speaking to the manager. If this does not resolve the matter a formal grievance can be made.

The employee must set out the formal grievance in writing and send it to the employer. The employer will then invite the employee to attend a meeting to discuss the grievance. The employee can be accompanied by a companion (usually a colleague or a trade union representative). The employer must then inform the employee of the decision and notify them of their right to appeal the decision.

# Chapter Summary

- There are a number of advantages to working in a team.

- There are a number or disadvantages to working in a team.

- Employees take on various roles within a team.

- There are various qualities a good team member should have.

- For a team to be effective it must have certain qualities.

- Conflicts can occur within a team and are due to certain conditions.

- Resolving conflict is an important skill for managers and team members alike.

- In serious cases a formal grievance procedure can be instigated.

# Practice Questions

## Chapter 9

**9.1**

Which of the following statements best describes a team in the workplace?

a)      A group of people working together without disagreements or conflict.

b)      The process of working collaboratively with a group of people in order to achieve a goal.

c)      A group of people with similar skills each of whom can do the other team members' jobs.

d)      A group of people who all have the same line manager.

**9.2**

Outline four possible advantages a team has over working individually.

**9.3**

Outline four possible disadvantages of working in a team.

**9.4**

List six qualities a team member should ideally possess for a team to function effectively.

**9.5**

Sushma works at the next desk to you. She is friendly and wants to share all her thoughts (every last one of them) with you. She isn't trying to cause problems for anyone but her incessant talking is just keeping you from concentrating on your work. How will you deal with the problem?

**9.6**

Your supervisor at work is constantly putting more demands on your time. New projects seem to be appearing daily and priorities seem to be changing by the hour. The only way to keep up is to work very long hours and even then your head is barely above water. How will you deal with the problem?

**9.7**

Your supervisor at work seems to have taken a dislike to you. He constantly blames you for problems that occur in the office, even if they are caused by others. He regularly gives you so much work that you find it impossible to meet deadlines without working excessive hours, and he has regularly threatened you with dismissal if you don't keep to the deadlines. How will you deal with the problem?

# Chapter 10

## Developing Skills and Knowledge

In this chapter we will see the need for continually developing skills and knowledge.

We shall look at how Continuing Professional Development (CPD) helps both in personal career ambitions and in meeting the current job role.

We shall see what can be considered as CPD.

We shall see the need for a Professional Development Plan (PDP).

We will look at recording CPD activities

All individuals will need to update their knowledge and skills relating to their professional lives. They will need to do this for two reasons:

- To manage their own learning and growth

- To meet the needs of the role within the organisation.

**Continuing Professional Development (CPD)**

Continuing professional development (CPD) is the means by which people maintain their knowledge and skills related to their professional lives. It covers a range of approaches, ideas and techniques which will help manage an individual's own learning and growth. CPD is necessary wherever an individual is in their career.

Gone are the days of high job security. In the past it was possible to have the same employer for life and automatically move up a well defined career ladder. This is not the case today. Workers nowadays are expected to gain career progression by learning new skills gaining new knowledge and they will need to be more mobile in finding suitable jobs.

Rapid advancement in technology and keeping up to date with accounting and financial procedures mean that employees need to upgrade and retrain simply to stand still in today's constantly changing world of work. If you don't learn the new skills you may become unemployable.

For membership of many professional bodies (such as the AAT) CPD is a requirment.

CPD isn't a fixed process. It can take the form of:

- Reading books or magazines.

- Attending courses.

- Writing presentations, articles or books.

- Delivering presentations.

- Undertaking further study, training or qualifications.

- Mentoring or shadowing other employees.

- Planning, organising or attending relevant events.

**Professional Development Plan**

Effective CPD will include a suitable Professional Development Plan (PDP). There are four stages in producing an effective PDP.

1. Identify the skills required to do your present job or to achieve your career objectives. Your job description may list the things you are expected to do, but you should also consider the skills you will need to develop you career in the future. It is useful to discuss your needs with your supervisor. Not only will you get a second opinion on what is needed, but you will also find that the supervisor will be more helpful when it comes to finding resources to help you (for example giving you time off to complete a training course). There will be short term goals (those which you need as soon as possible) and long term goals (those which you will need in your future career).

2. Then you should look at your list and ask yourself how effectively you match against each one. It is important to be honest about your answers. Are there areas which would benefit from more confidence? Are there areas where you feel confident at the moment but would be even greater strengths with some development?

3. Identify what you need to do to achieve the gaps or developments listed in 2 above. These are the objectives and should adhere to the S.M.A R.T. principles (see p 106). Particularly you need to be specific. For example, it is much more helpful to say "I need to learn how to use 'Outlook' to sort, prioritise and store my emails", than it is to say "I need to be more organised".

4. Review the progress regularly. This is essential. You need to know what has been achived and what hasn't. You must analyse the value of what you have done and identify where more development is needed. A review should take place every 3, 6 or 12 months with your supervisor or whoever has helped to develop you PDP.

# CHAPTER 10
## Developing Skills and Knowledge

Some professional bodies specify a certain number of hours which must be carried out by their members each year. However, time spent on CPD is not so important as gaining the required skills and knowledge to enable the individual to perform at the top of their abilities.

## Recording CPD

It is important to record your CPD activities. Many professionals need to formally record their CPD to meet the requirements of their employer or Professional Institution. However, recording CPD can be useful for a number of reasons other than for meeting the requirements of others. It can play a key part in the planning and reviewing of CPD activities, as well as providing a useful source when updating Curriculum Vitae or making a case for promotion.

There is no set form of how to record CPD activities, but some professional bodies provide templates and forms which may be selected for viewing by the body. Typically they will include:

- The CPD goal. What it is you have identified as a need.

- What you identified as how to achieve the goal. This may be a course you went on or the study you undertook.

- The date you undertook the activity.

- Why you undertook the activity. An explanation of how it would help towards achieving your goal.

- How effective the activity was. What did you learn from the course or study?

- How you have used what you learnt or how you will use it in the future.

- Any further action needed to achieve the goal. Was the activity successful in achieving the goal or do you need further actions?

Every person will have differing needs and goals, so there cannot be a single PDP plan which will be useful to everyone or even small groups of people. You must remember that a PDP is unique to each person.

CPD is an investment that an individual makes in him/herself. It's a way of planning individual development that links learning directly to practice. CPD can help a person keep skills up to date, and prepare them for greater responsibilities. It can boost confidence, strengthen professional credibility and help employees become more creative in tackling new challenges. CPD makes working life more interesting and can significantly increase job satisfaction. It can accelerate career development and is an important part of achieving career goals and ambitions.

## Chapter Summary

- The present day working environment has a need for continually updating skills and knowledge.

- Continuing Professional Development (CPD) is the way this is achieved.

- There are many types of CPD activities.

- CPD should be constantly planned by using a Personal Development Plan (PDP).

- CPD activities should be regularly recorded and assessed as to how useful they have been.

# **Practice Questions**

## **Chapter 10**

### **10.1**

Which statement best describes CPD (Continuing Professional Development)?

a) A list of courses you have attended throughout the year.

b) A list of skills needed to complete the job.

c) A means by which people maintain their knowledge and skills related to their professional lives.

d) An assessment of what you need to do to get a promotion.

### **10.2**

Which of the following can be considered as suitable CPD activities?

a) Attending a one day course on Financial Planning.

b) Helping plan a work project.

c) Researching new computer programs to do with accounting and finance.

d) Surfing the internet for items about the economy.

e) Acting as office manager while the regular manager is away on holiday.

f) Gaining a new qualification in spreadsheet software, but this isn't part of your job description.

g) Reading the Accounting Technician magazine.

h) Looking after a new employee and showing them the company's working practices.

i) Delivering a presentation to managers on how to reduce costs in the workplace.

j) Attending a seminar organised by the AAT.

# CHAPTER 10
## Developing Skills and Knowledge

**10.3**

Who should be involved in creating and reviewing a Personal Development Plan (PDP)?

a) The office manager should organise and review the PDP.

b) The individual should organise and review their own PCP.

c) The professional body should organise and review the PDP.

d) The individual should discuss with the office manager what the PDP should consist of and how successful (or otherwise) it has been.

**10.4**

Create you own CPD plan for the next 12 months. You should include an assessment of what you need in your present position at work, what your present skills cover, and what you will need to cover gaps in your skills. You should also list the resources and help you will need from your present workplace (such as funding or cover for absence).

If you are not in work, carry out a similar exercise based on what you will need to get a suitable position. Resources may include funding, grants or childcare.

# Answers to Practice Questions

## Chapter 1

**1.1**

i)      a

ii)     c

iii)    b

**1.2**

1)      Recording sales

2)      Recording purchases

3)      Recording cash in and cash out.

(Other answers may be acceptable)

**1.3**

i)      c

ii)     a

iii)    b

**1.4**

Finance involves providing and managing funds and resources for an organisation. It checks the funds available and advises how best to use them. Accounting is for recording, analysing and reporting financial transactions and the company's financial position.

**1.5**

Internal auditors are employed by, or contracted to a business. They check that the company's policies and procedures are being followed.

The external auditor is independent of the entity being audited. They check that the financial transactions have been recorded accurately and in accordance with legal requirements.

**1.6**

a)      Sole Trader

b)      Limited Company

c)      Partnership

d)      Public Sector Organisation

e)      Co-operative

f)      Franchise

g)      Public Limited Company (plc)

**1.7**

i)      b

ii)      c

iii)      a

# ANSWERS TO PRACTICE QUESTIONS

**1.8**

a) Sales Ledger Clerk to Financial Accountant
Cashier to Financial Accountant
Payroll Clerk to Financial Accountant

b) Sales Ledger Clerk

c) Cashier

d) The Payroll Clerk first. Then if there was still a problem the Financial Accountant.

e) Purchases Ledger Clerk


**1.9**

a) A business owned or controlled by the government (or local government).

b) The owner(s) of a limited company

c) A person or organisation that has an interest in the financial performance of a business

d) A business run not to make a profit, but to address a social need.

e) A limited company which offers its shares to the general public.

## Chapter 2

**2.1**

(c)

**2.2**

(b)

**2.3**

(d)

**2.4**

(a)

To do nothing would suggest you are not really bothered about when the debt is paid

To present a winding up order to the court at this stage would be 'heavy-handed' and not in the interests of your company. If the company is liquidated there is every chance that you would not receive anything, since you would be last in priority. You may also have to pay court costs. Winding up orders are only as a very last resort.

A debt collection agency is premature. The invoice may simply have been overlooked. If this is the case then employing a debt collection agency would result in bad feeling and the customer is likely to go elsewhere for future goods or services. Employing a debt collector may be necessary, but only after you have established that the customer is purposely not paying.

The company should have a policy on what courses of action to follow when a customer has not paid their invoice and when each of the increasingly demanding actions should be taken.

**2.5**

It must be complete, accurate and timely.

**2.6**

1)	Sales Ledger (a list of credit customers with details of the amounts owing and amounts paid).

2)	Purchases Ledger (a list of credit suppliers with details of the amounts owing and amounts paid).

3)	Cash book (details of all the cash transactions of a company)

4)	Cash flow forecast (a prediction of all cash coming into the business and all cash going out of the business)

5)	A bank reconciliation (a document which explains the difference between the balance on the bank statement and the balance on the cash book).

(Only 3 answers required, but other answers are possible)

**2.7**

(b)

**2.8**

An individual, a sole trader or a partner in a partnership who is insolvent can go bankrupt; a limited company which is insolvent can go into liquidation.

# ANSWERS TO PRACTICE QUESTIONS

## Chapter 3

**3.1**     c

**3.2**     d

**3.3**     c

**3.4**     All the statements are true

**3.5**     a) only

**3.6**     None are true

**3.7**     c) only

**3.8**     a

**3.9**     c

**3.10**    c and d

## Chapter 4

**4.1**

a) , b), c) and f)

**4.2**

a)     Integrity

b)     Professional Behaviour

c)     Objectivity

d)     Professional Competence and Due Care

e)     Confidentiality

f)     Professional Competence and Due Care

**4.3**

| Scenario | Breach of principle (Yes/No) | Principle Breached |
|---|---|---|
| The business you work for wants a new trainee and has advertised for a person under the age of 25. | Yes | Equality |
| Your brother has just started a new business selling stationery to local businesses. You suggest that your company uses this business but you don't tell them that the owner is your brother. | Yes | Objectivity |
| A friend of yours has just been told that she is to inherit a substantial amount of money from a long lost relative who has just died. Your friend asks if you will deal with the inheritance tax details. You don't know much about inheritance tax but you agree because she is your friend. | Yes | Professional Competence and Due Care |
| You suspect that one of your clients is using the profits from his business to fund terrorist activities. You tell the police of your suspicions. | No | (It is in the public interest to disclose) |
| You are keen to get the job advertised in the jobs pages of an internet site. You decide to amend your CV to say that you are AAT qualified even though you have still to complete the last two units. | Yes | Professional Behaviour |
| Your boss asks you to understate the value of stock held in the warehouse in order to artificially reduce the profit shown in the Statement of Profit or Loss. You refuse | No | (This is the right thing to do) |

**4.4**

Which of the following statements are true?

a)    Sustainability involves selling cheap, inferior goods to make most profit

False. Sustainable goods are often more expensive but certainly not inferior.

b)    Sustainability involves seeking materials and products from suppliers where the employees are paid a fair wage even though these may be more expensive than from another supplier.

True

c)    Sustainability involves funding your staff to study for the AAT qualification

True.

d)      Sustainability involves sponsoring local community projects so that planning permission for your new factory will go ahead more smoothly.

Partly true. Sponsoring the local community is true, but for the wrong reason.

e)      Sustainability involves taking your staff out for a Christmas Party.

True. This is 'bonding'.


## 4.5

a)      Having a fire drill at regular intervals.

This is a policy for Health and Safety, but not sustainability

b)      Offering work experience places for children from the local school.

This is a sustainability policy supporting the local community

c)      Putting up a notice reminding people to switch off the lights if they are the last one in the office.

This is a sustainability policy reducing the 'carbon footprint'.

d)      Keeping an accident book

This is a policy for Health and Safety, but not sustainability

e)      Putting up a Health & Safety Poster

This is a policy for Health and Safety, but not sustainability

f)      Having an annual open day for the general public.

This is a sustainability policy supporting the local community.

## Chapter 5

**5.1**

£3.99 - £2.65 = £1.34 so the % reduction is (1.34/3.99) x 100 = 33.6% to 1 d.p.

**5.2**

£420 x 5% (or 5 / 100) = £21.        £420 + £21 = £441.

**5.3**

£600 x 15% = £90.        £600 - £90 = £510

**5.4**

£45 is 80% of the original price. So £45 / 80 x 100 = £56.25

**5.5**

£217.35 is 115% of the cost price.

£217.35 / 115 x 100 = £189.00

**5.6**

|  | 2013 £ | % | 2014 £ | % |
|---|---|---|---|---|
| Sales | 2,350,000 | 100 | 2,560,000 | 100 |
| Cost of Sales | 940,000 | 40.0 | 1,075,200 | 42.0 |
| Gross Profit | 1,410,000 | 60.0 | 1,484,800 | 58.0 |
| Wages and Salaries | 400,000 | 17.02 | 486,000 | 18.98 |
| General Office Costs | 200,000 | 8.51 | 243,000 | 9.49 |
| Total Overheads | 600,000 | 25.53 | 729,000 | 28.48 |
| Net Profit | 810,000 | 34.47 | 755,800 | 29.52 |

**5.7**

|  | 2013 £'000 | 2014 £'000 |
|---|---|---|
| Sales | 2,350 | 2,560 |
| Cost of Sales | 940 | 1,075 |
| Gross Profit | 1,410 | 1,485 |
| Wages and Salaries | 400 | 486 |
| General Office Costs | 200 | 243 |
| Total Overheads | 600 | 729 |
| Net Profit | 810 | 756 |

**Task 5.8**

**Mean**

$36 + 35 + 31 + 41 + 30 + 37 + 29 + 32 + 36 + 33 + 32 + 35 + 37 + 30 + 36 = 510$

$510 \div 15 = \mathbf{34}$

**Median**

The figures arranged in ascending order are:

29, 30, 30, 31, 32, 32, 33, 35, 35, 36, 36, 36, 37, 37, 41.

The middle figure is the $8^{th}$ figure which is **35**

**Mode**

The figure which occurs most frequently is **36** (3 times)

## Chapter 6

**6.1**

| GREENS GARDEN CENTRES Sales by Branch | | | | |
|---|---|---|---|---|
| | **2011** **£'000s** | **2012** **£'000** | **2013** **£'000** | **2014** **£'000** |
| Dundee Branch | 470 | 580 | 650 | 705 |
| Wilmslow Branch | 120 | 295 | 410 | 470 |
| Slough Branch | 410 | 350 | 295 | 350 |
| Torquay Branch | 175 | 235 | 295 | 300 |

There may be variations in the layout of the table, but the essential features are
- Title showing what the data is about
- Branches clearly shown
- The year and the units of currency clearly shown
- The data should be clear and unambiguous

**6.2**

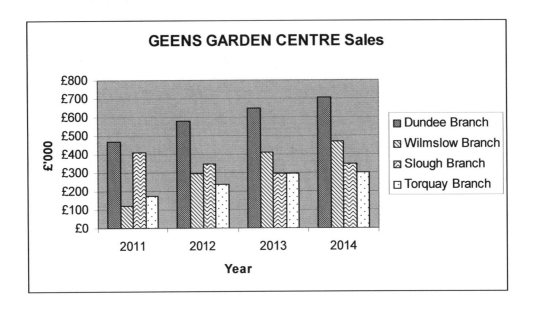

Essential elements are
- Title
- Axes labels
- Key
- Suitable scale with equal increments

**6.3**

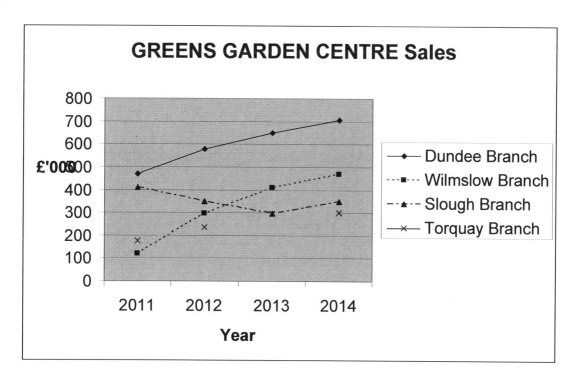

Dundee and Wilmslow sales have a similar upward trend. Torquay has an upward trend but not as good as Dundee and Wilmslow and has been relatively flat over the last year. Slough has shown a downward trend but has recovered a little in 2014.

**6.4**

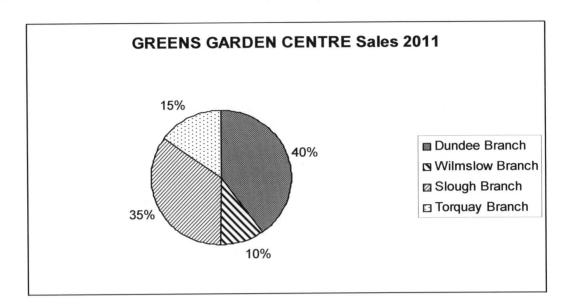

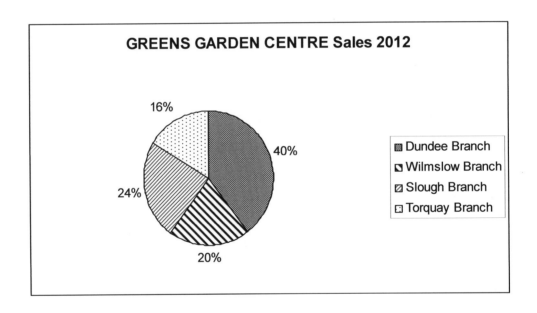

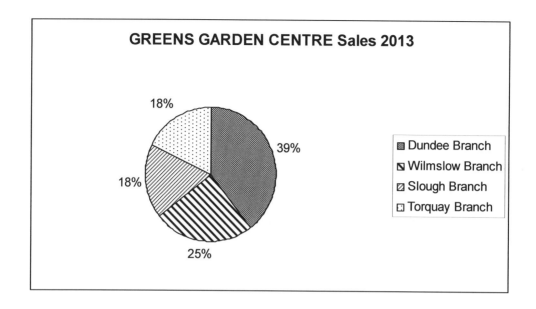

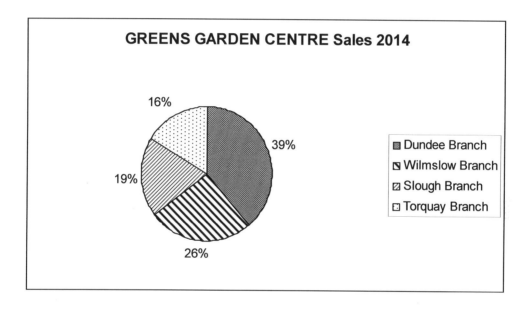

## Chapter 7

**7.1**

a)

'Cc' stands for 'carbon copy' and it tells you that a copy of the memo has gone to this person.

'Bcc' stands for 'blind carbon copy' whereby the recipient is not made aware that a copy has been sent to anyone else.

b)

Fax (or scan it and send as an attachment to an email).

**7.2**

---

**DAWSON SUPPLIES**

**45 Scartho Street,**
**Immingham,**
**IM15 2BH**


T&T
154 Margaret Street,
Immingham,
IM17 9RQ

1$^{st}$ May 2014

Dear Mr Singh:

Overdue order

We understand that there has been a delay in processing your order for 20 rolls of fabric. We apologise for the delay but have discovered that we only received the Purchase Order 2 days ago.


We will endeavour to process this order as soon as possible and it should be with you no later than the middle of next week. Please be assured that your order will be treated as a priority.


I am enclosing a copy of the purchase order


Yours sincerely



Mr A Student

Encl.   Copy purchase order

---

(Students are not expected to have exactly the same words, but essential features are the layout, naming the recipient, politeness, concise, the salutation (Yours sincerely) and stating the enclosures if there are any. There should be no blame placed on T&T)

**7.3**

---

To:     **Richard Bray, Managing Director**

From: **(Your name), Accounts Assistant**

Date:  **21st January 2015**

Report:        **The Importance of Health and Safety in the Accounts Office.**

**Introduction**

On 21st January a report was requested by you on the importance of Health and Safety in the Accounts Office. It was to be completed by 31st January 2015.

**The reasons for maintaining a Health and Safety policy.**

The workplace should be a safe place. Most people do not want to work in an environment where their life is in danger. Even in dangerous occupations, the employee will want to know that the risks have been assessed and measures taken to reduce the risks as much as possible.

According to the Health and Safety Executive (HSE) over 200 people a year lose their lives at work in Britain and an estimated 2 million suffer from ill health caused or made worse by work. Many accidents at work can be prevented by a little forethought and planning.

Implementing health and safety measures doesn't have to be expensive or time consuming. In fact, safer and more efficient working practices can save money, as well as save lives.

Not only is a Health and Safety Policy beneficial to the employee, in that it will help to prevent accidents and ill health at work; it will also benefit the employer in that fewer days off work will be taken and working practices will become more efficient. It will also help prevent claims for compensation.

**A summary of legal requirements.**

There are many laws covering Health and Safety but the main piece of legislation is the Health and Safety at Work Act 1974. This sets out the general duties which an employer has towards his/her employees and the general public. It requires employers of five or more people to have a written statement of health and safety policy. The Act also sets out the responsibilities of the employees in keeping themselves safe and helping maintaining a safe workplace.
Another piece of legislation requires that employers display an approved poster in the workplace. These are obtainable from HSE.

---

A further piece of legislation requires that all businesses with 10 or more employees keep a record of all accidents at work. Accident books are also available from HSE.

It is a legal requirement that a fire risk assessment is carried out, escape routes are clearly marked, fire fighting equipment is available, and the staff is trained in fire safety and what to do in the event of a fire.

It is also a legal requirement that a risk assessment is made of computers and monitors used by the staff. Staff should be allowed regular breaks and be allowed a free eye test when they request one.

There are other pieces of legislation covering Health and Safety; some are specific to certain industries (such as coal mining and oil drilling). The employer should take steps to ensure that the Health and Safety Policy is complete and enforced. The employer can either do this him/herself or can delegate a responsible person to carry out this duty on the employer's behalf.

**Health and Safety policy over and above the legal requirements.**

While much of a Health and Safety Policy will be covered by legislation, the risk assessment may highlight further areas which can be made safer. A Health and Safety Policy should take a common sense approach. The employer must think about what Health and Safety means to the business. Policies should address risks but not be so restrictive as to go beyond common sense. A Health and Safety Policy should aid working practices and not prevent them.

The risk assessment should be viewed not only in terms of what is legally required, but also in terms of what aids the employees and the business. The steps taken to ensure Health and Safety should be proportionate to the risk. It is disproportionate to ban the use of an essential piece of equipment because someone may bruise themselves if not used properly, but it is proportionate to ensure that staff is trained in the safe use of the equipment.

A Health and Safety Policy should cover all the legal requirements as also go further to ensure that risks to safety and health are cut to a minimum.

**The consequences of not complying with the legal requirements.**

Local authorities operate in partnership with HSE to ensure that Health & Safety legislation is upheld. They have the right to inspect premises and working activities to ensure that the business is complying with the legislation. Inspections may be unannounced. The local authority or the HSE may also follow up complaints by staff or members of the public.
If the local authority or HSE find breaches of the law, they have a range of options. They may offer advice either face to face or in writing. They may issue improvement or prohibition orders. The business will be forced to improve its working practices or conditions or even prevented from carrying out these activities until improvements have been made.

In the most serious of cases the local authority or HSE may decide to prosecute. If found guilty, the business, the person responsible for Health and Safety, the managers, or the directors can face an unlimited fine and/or up to two years imprisonment. Directors who are found guilty can be disqualified from holding such a position for up to 15 years.

Businesses or individuals who are convicted in the courts for serious breaches of Health and Safety laws will have their names published in the media.

(Students may not give as detailed an answer as shown above, and they may not have access to the sources of information required in real situations. However, the informal report should cover the main points and the source of information can be from this book at the very least. Attention should be given to the title, and the subheadings. Spelling, grammar and use of English are all features which will be assessed)

**7.4**

---

TWO WHEELS

37 South Street,
Salisbury,
SP2 3EQ

On Your Bike
127 St Martin's Street,
Ipswich,
IP1 RQ

2<sup>nd</sup> June 2015

Dear Mr Jamal

<u>Re Delivery Note 26980</u>

We have received the goods as per the copy delivery note (see enclosed), but you will see from the purchase order (copy also enclosed) that we have received the wrong colour.

We would appreciate you earliest attention to this with a delivery of the bikes of the correct colour, at which time we will return the incorrect items.

Yours sincerely

*A Student*

A Student
Accounts Assistant

Enc     Copy Purchase Order
        Copy Delivery Note

---

It is not necessary to have the letter word for word but essential features are the layout, naming the recipient, politeness, concise, the salutation (Yours sincerely) and stating the enclosures. There should be no blame placed on 'On Your Bike'.

**7.5**

# Memorandum

**To:**     A Khan

**cc:**     V Symanski

**From:**   A Student

**Date:**   2nd June 2015

**Re:**     Delivery of Cruiser Bicycles

---

The delivery of the cruiser bicycles received yesterday was of the wrong colour.

'On Your Bike' will be coming with the correct colour (red) and taking back the wrong colour (blue).

I will keep you informed as to the time and date when 'On Your Bike' informs me

Students should have the correct format and the correct information in a concise manner.

**7.6**

a) Assuming you have the authority to reply to such an email, a return email would be acceptable. You can return an email with an email.

b) You will need to sent the branch manager a fax, or alternatively you could scan a copy and email it as an attachment

c) You can send a memo to all staff. If you have a group email address you could email everyone.

d) Assuming you have the authority to reply to such a letter, you should return a letter with a letter.

e) A simple note would be suitable.

## Chapter 8

**8.1**

a)


**8.2**

b)


**8.3**

c)


**8.4**

The aim is most likely to be to maximise profits

The objectives will be a), c), and e).

d) appears to be an objective for another aim.


**8.5**

a), c) and d)

b) is neither specific, measurable or timely

e) is not specific or measurable

It could be argued that c) is not specific or measurable. However, it is measurable as it will be for the entire brand and it is specific in that it is different from the old.

**8.6**

a)   1

b)   1

c)   3

d)   2

e)   4

f)   1

g)   2

h)   3

i)   3

j)   1

**8.7**

b), c) and e)

## Chapter 9

**9.1**

b)

**9.2**

Four from:

- Pooling skills.

- Stimulate creative thinking.

- Increased energy and enthusiasm

- Speed up the job as different members can do different parts of the job at the same time.

- Deciding on the correct course of action or method quicker by asking for advice from other team members

- In creased motivation due to support from other team members.

Note: Other answers are possible.

**9.3**

Four from:

- Some team members can sit back and let others do the work.

- It may take longer to prepare the work as strategies and work plans must be discussed and agreed.

- Some people find it difficult to work in a team as they don't like to share the work. They like to be active in all parts of a project.

- Some workers may limit their creativity in order to fall in line with the ideas of other team members.

- There is likely to be conflict between team members.

- Team members may go against their better judgement due to presser from others in the team.

Note: Other answers are possible.

**9.4**

Six from:

- Being reliable

- Being a good communicator

- Being a good listener

- Being an active member (rather than a passive member)

- Willingness to share ideas an information

- Willingness to work together and help other team members

- Ability to accept and adapt to change

- Being a committed member of the team

- Being able to solve problems

- Be respectful and supportive to other team members.

Note: Other answers are possible.

**9.5**

Rather than risk insulting Sushma, put the blame on yourself. Tell her you have trouble concentrating while you are listening to her very interesting stories. You'd love to hear them at some other time, just not while you're working.

If this doesn't make any difference you should speak to your supervisor in confidence. Your supervisor may be able to come up with some reason for reorganising the seating in the office.

Note: Other answers are possible, but you should ensure that you do not insult Sushma or alienate her in any way.

**9.6**

The best way to address this situation is to have a talk with the supervisor. Have a prepared list of every project you have going and where it is at in terms of being finished.

Explain how you prioritised the list and what you feel are the most important projects to complete before taking on more.

If the supervisor wants to add more to your list, give them an honest assessment as to when it can be started.

If they insist it must be started earlier, ask them which project on this list should be discarded or postponed.

The idea is to bring to their reality all of the commitments so they can understand the volume of work on your plate. You need to be firm when stating that you simply cannot take on another project until the present ones are finished. Explain that it is far better to have one job done well than 20 jobs done poorly.

This type of supervisor often does not realise the extent of your frustration until you discuss it so it may come as a shock when you finally draw the line.

Don't be obstructive. Try to come to some agreement as to how the jobs can get done, but at the same time the supervisor must be realistic in his/her demands.

It is important to keep calm and courteous. You must not be seen as being objectionable as well as obstructive. If you become angry or personal in your objections the supervisor will become defensive and will probably not see your point of view.

If the supervisor won't change his/her position, even after the facts have been discussed, you may wish to refer the matter to a higher authority.

Note: Other answers are possible, but you should try to solve the problem informally first and you should ensure that you remain calm and courteous.

**9.7**

This amounts to bullying. This is a serious problem and you should follow the company grievance procedure. It will suggest that you try to resolve the matter informally first. This will involve talking to the supervisor, or to someone else such as a trade union official or someone in the Human Resources department.

If this doesn't resolve the matter, a formal grievance should be made. You should send a letter to your employer setting out the details of the complaint. The employer must then arrange a meting with you to discuss the matter. The employer must then inform you what action (if any) they intend to take. You have a right to appeal this decision.

If all the grievance procedures have been exhausted you can take your claim to an employment tribunal.

## Chapter 10

**10.1**

c)

**10.2**

All of them

**10.3**

d)

**10.4**

The answers will vary depending on the circumstances of the student. The plan should demonstrate an understanding of the stages involved in creating a PDP and the objectives should be realistic in both content and timeframe.

**Practice Assessment**

**for**

**AAT Level 2 Certificate**

# Work Effectively in Accounting and Finance

PRACTICE ASSESSMENT

**Scenario**

You are **Sophie Bradley**. You have just started working for **Kemp Foods** as an accounts clerk. Kemp Foods has been expanding its sales market and as a result has created two new posts; an Accounts Clerk (you) and a Payroll Clerk.

Kemp Foods specialises in frozen ready meals. It has just secured a new contract with Asco Supermarkets to supply a range of products. This has meant that more production staff have been recruited along with the two new posts of Accounts Clerk and Payroll Clerk.

Jess Clarke is your line manager, but you can also expect requests for work from Bonnie Horwood and Tyrone Thompson. Requests for work will be completed on a work request form and should be received by 12.00 on a Friday for work to be completed the following week. That way you can plan your work for the following week and identify any issues. Jess has set aside an hour each Monday morning at 09.00 to go through your work schedule and discuss any problems.

Your hours of work are 09.00 to 17.00 Monday to Friday with an hour for lunch which can be taken at any time between 12.00 and 14.00. If you are really busy you can work an hour's overtime in the evening but this is subject to approval by Jess Clarke. No further overtime is possible as the offices are locked at 18.00.

This post (and the payroll clerk's post) is a brand new post and so Joe Anyon, the Senior Financial Accountant, will be taking a keen interest in how the job is going. He may ask for a report from you or Jess from time to time.

Kemp Foods are paying for you to complete the AAT course. Joe Anyon will review any further requests for staff training and development. He has a review meeting with each member of staff once every three months, with a formal appraisal every year. At the three month review meeting any problems will be discussed and training needs identified.

You have undergone an induction for the first week of your employment with Jess Clarke. She has explained the routine tasks you are to carry out on a weekly basis. However, since the company is so busy, much of the time is spent getting on with jobs on your own initiative. Jess has asked you to keep a list of any problems or things you don't understand and she will go through them at the end of the day if necessary.

All internal email addresses follow the same format. There is the person's first initial, dot, last name @ kempfoods.com. So your email address is s.bradley@kempfoods.com .

Today's Date is Friday 29th June and you have been at Kemp Foods for 4 weeks.

# Kemp Foods

# Organisation Chart

# Accounts Department

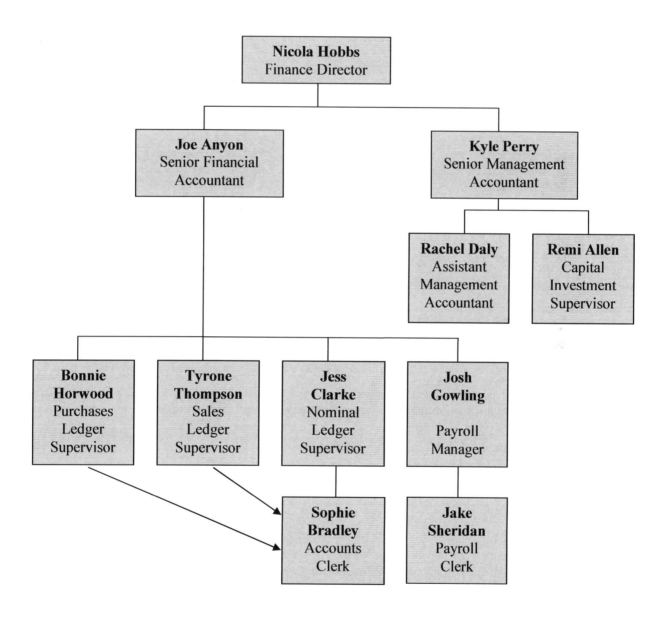

# Job Description

# Sophie Bradley

**Job Title:**   Accounts Clerk

**Salary**   £12,500 - £14,500

**Reports to**   Jess Clarke

## Responsibilities

- To undertake day to day functions of the accounts department such as answering the telephone, dealing with enquiries from customers and suppliers and taking messages.

- Provide administrative and clerical support to Purchase Ledger Supervisor, Sales Ledger Supervisor and Nominal Ledger Supervisor.

- To undertake work as requested by Purchase Ledger Supervisor, Sales Ledger Supervisor and Nominal Ledger Supervisor.

- Attend training to develop relevant knowledge and skills.

- Input accounts data into the computerised accounts system.

- Maintain confidentiality in all aspects of work.

| Person Specification Sophie Bradley | | |
|---|---|---|
| | **Essential Criteria** | **Desirable Criteria** |
| **Qualifications** | A relevant IT qualification. | 5 GCSE's or equivalent including mathematics and English. |
| **Experience** | • Experience of maintaining and developing spreadsheets.<br>• Experience of business letter writing. | • Experience of dealing with customers.<br>• Previous experience of office work |
| **Creativity** | • Ability to work on own initiative.<br>• Ability to work on a number of tasks.<br>• Accurate and thorough approach.<br>• Ability to organise and prioritise own work schedule. | Ability to create informal business reports. |
| **People Skills** | • Quick and enthusiastic learner.<br>• Professional communication skills with both businesses and other colleagues.<br>• Knowledge and understanding of working in a team.<br>• An understanding of confidentiality | Past experience of working in a team. |
| **Circumstances** | • Able to work Monday to Friday between 9am and 5pm.<br>• Be in good general health. | Willingness to work occasional extra hours between 5pm and 6pm. |

# Kemp Foods

# Work Request

# from

# Jess Clarke

| Task Code | Task | Estimated time | Date and time required for completion |
|-----------|------|----------------|----------------------------------------|
| JC1 | Meet with Jess to discuss work schedule. | 1 hour | Monday 2nd July 10am |
| JC2 | Collect, open and distribute post | 1 hour | Every day before 12pm (midday) |
| JC3 | Complete the bank reconciliation and prepare a list of uncashed cheques. | 4 hours | Wednesday 4th July 5pm |
| JC4 | Prepare journals according to the figures supplied by Rachel Daly and send to Joe Anyon for authorisation. | 6 hours | Wednesday 4th July 5pm |
| JC5 | Collect the petty cash vouchers and listings from each department and enter them onto the computer. Process requests for top up. | 3 hours | Friday 6th July 5pm |
| JC6 | Input the journals you prepared in JC4 onto the computer once they have been authorised. | 2 hours | Friday 6th July 5pm |
| JC7 | Send email regarding Annual Food and Drink conference to all managers and supervisors. | 1 hour | Thursday 5th July 5pm |
| JC8 | Collect money from all staff for National Lottery Syndicate. | 1 hour | Friday 6th July 12pm (midday) |
| JC9 | Prepare work schedule | 1 hour | Friday 6th July 5pm |

# Kemp Foods

# Work Request

# from

# Tyrone Thompson

| Task Code | Task | Estimated time | Date and time required for completion |
|---|---|---|---|
| TT1 | Assist Production Manager to show the new customers around the factory. Customers arrive at 1pm on Thursday. | 2 hours | Thursday 5th July 3pm |
| TT2 | Print off an Aged Debtor Analysis and contact those over 60 days overdue. Request payment ASAP and record response. | 4 hours | Tuesday 3rd July 5pm |
| TT3 | Input list of monies paid by debtors onto computer and prepare documentation for banking. | 2 hours | Monday 2nd July before 5pm |
| TT4 | Collate Sales Ledger reports and send to regional sales managers | 3 hours | Monday 9th July before 12pm (midday) |

# Kemp Foods

# Work Request

# from

# Bonnie Horwood

| Task Code | Task | Estimated time | Date and time required for completion |
|---|---|---|---|
| BH1 | Check Supplier invoices with Goods Received notes. | 2 hours | Thursday 5th July 5pm |
| BH2 | Print off list of outstanding invoices. Select those suppliers due for payment and prepare payment documentation. | 5 hours | Tuesday 3rd July 5pm |

# Kemp Foods

## Petty Cash Procedures

- A petty cash float of £150 is managed by a nominated manager for each department to cover minor items of expenditure where the normal purchasing procedure is not viable or value for money.

- Under no circumstances should petty cash be used for the payment of salaries, wages, staff travelling or subsistence. Petty cash must not be borrowed or used for personal purposes, for cashing personal cheques or for purposes outside a valid Kemp Foods business purpose.

- Petty cash must be held in a lockable cash box. The cash box should be kept in the departmental safe at all times. Keys to the cash box and safe must be kept in a separate, secure place by the nominated manager. A duplicate set of keys will be kept by the Finance Director.

- All requests for monies from petty cash should be made to the nominated manager. All payments from petty cash must be properly recorded on the blue voucher, stating the amount given. The voucher must also give details of the purchase and the reason for payment. The voucher must be signed by the nominated manager. A valid receipt must be attached to all vouchers. Payment can only be made if a corresponding receipt is available. Petty cash should not be used for items in excess of £50.

- The petty cash will be reimbursed weekly on Monday morning provided listings of payments along with vouchers and receipts are provided by 12pm Friday.

- A breach of any of these procedures may result in disciplinary action.

PRACTICE ASSESSMENT

## ASSESSMENT TASKS

## PART 1

**Task 1.1**

One of your weekly tasks is to collect information from Rachel Daly. Explain what type of information this may be.

| Answer |
|---|
|  |

**Task 1.2**

Why might this information be useful for Kemp Foods to become more efficient and remain solvent?

| Answer |
|---|
|  |

**Task 1.3**

Kemp Foods is covered by organisational procedures and legal requirements. Give two examples of areas required to be covered by legislation and two areas which are common policies but not covered by legislation. (Ensure you identify which is which).

| **Answer** |
| --- |
| <br><br><br><br><br><br><br><br><br><br> |

**Task 1.4**

Your immediate line manager is Jess Clarke. However, you will need to liaise with other office staff. Say to whom you would refer the following issues:

a)    You feel you need further training on spreadsheets to complete your work efficiently.

Name ………………………………………………..

b)    A supplier has contacted you concerning a new computer system for the company.

Name ………………………………………………..

c)      The weekly payroll data has been sent but is not complete.

Name    ………………………………………..

d)      You receive a phone call from the salesperson saying they want some petty cash but the sales manager, who is the person responsible for petty cash, is away on holiday and there is no key.

Name    ………………………………………..

e)      A customer has phoned regarding a delivery of some goods with damaged packaging.

Name    ………………………………………..

**1.5**

During your first few weeks at Kemp Foods you have noticed that company policy regarding petty cash has not been followed in a number of cases. The blue petty cash voucher has been missing, with a signature scrawled on the receipt instead. There have been two cases where there has been an IOU found amongst the receipts.

Jess Clarke has asked you to prepare an email which can be sent to all departments explaining why it is important to follow the procedures and the consequences if they are not. You should send the email to Jess only at first for her approval.

(Use the next page for your answer).

PRACTICE ASSESSMENT

**From:**

**To:**

**Date:**

**Subject:**

**1.6**

Review the work request forms from Jess Clarke, Tyrone Thompson and Bonnie Horwood and complete the work schedule below. Identify tasks where you will have difficulty meeting the deadline and identify tasks you will have to carry forward to the following week. (Don't forget to allow yourself a lunch break)

|  | Monday 2nd July | Tuesday 3rd July | Wednesday 4th July | Thursday 5th July | Friday 6th July |
|---|---|---|---|---|---|
| 9.00 – 10.00 |  |  |  |  |  |
| 10.00 – 11.00 |  |  |  |  |  |
| 11.00 – 12.00 |  |  |  |  |  |
| 12.00 – 13.00 |  |  |  |  |  |
| 13.00 – 14.00 |  |  |  |  |  |
| 14.00 – 15.00 |  |  |  |  |  |
| 15.00 – 16.00 |  |  |  |  |  |
| 16.00 – 17.00 |  |  |  |  |  |
| Possible 17.00 – 18.00 |  |  |  |  |  |

Problems identified (if any)

**1.7**

Tyrone Thompson has spent many years at Kemp Foods and he has learnt most of what he knows through doing the job and learning through experience. He has little time for formal training, particularly when it takes staff away from their work in the office. He has no formal qualifications and tries to avoid going on courses and attending training as much as possible.

He has heard that you have been given a morning off next month to take your AAT exam at the local college. He is not pleased. He feels it is a waste of time and you would be much better learning how to do the job you've got rather than 'waste your time at college learning stuff you won't need at work'. He has also made it clear that he feels that while you are away, the rest of the office will have to cover your work, which is an unnecessary added pressure.

What difficulties do you anticipate in your working relationship with Tyrone? Suggest ways you could resolve them.

**Answer**

PRACTICE ASSESSMENT

## PART 2

The scenario is the same as for part 1 except that the time has moved on. It is now **Friday 3rd August**.

**2.1**

Joe Anyon is pleased at how the business is growing after the new contract with Asco, but he would like a few facts and figures to take with him to a meeting next week with Nicola Hobbs, the Finance Director.

Joe is particularly interested in the relationship between the staff costs and sales. He has asked Josh Gowling to provide you with some figures from the payroll.

There are three grades of production workers, A, B and C. You have been given the following payroll information for May, June and July.

| | | Total payroll costs for May £ | Total payroll costs for June £ | Total payroll costs for July £ |
|---|---|---|---|---|
| Grade A | Basic hours pay | 93,513 | 118,300 | 113,793 |
| | Overtime | 35,068 | 17,745 | 24,505 |
| Grade B | Basic hours pay | 26,000 | 28,600 | 27,300 |
| | Overtime | 9,750 | 4,290 | 6,240 |
| Grade C | Basic hours pay | 7,367 | 8,840 | 8,840 |
| | Overtime | 2,763 | 1,326 | 1,657 |

| Number of Staff | | | |
|---|---|---|---|
| | **May** | **June** | **July** |
| Grade A | 83 | 105 | 101 |
| Grade B | 20 | 22 | 21 |
| Grade C | 5 | 6 | 6 |

Joe has also asked you to retrieve the sales figures for May June and July from the computer. The figures are as follows:

| Sales | | |
|---|---|---|
| May | June | July |
| £ | £ | £ |
| 1,153,843 | 1,442,304 | 1,413,458 |

196

# PRACTICE ASSESSMENT

Joe wants you to calculate the following:

a) The average pay per person for each grade for each month and the average pay per person in total for each month.

b) The percentage of overtime pay in relation to total pay for each month across all grades.

c) The average sales per employee for each month.

**(Round your monetary figures to pounds and whole pence and percentages to two decimal places).**

**Workings for a)**

**May**

| | Total Pay £ | Number of Employees | Average pay £ |
|---|---|---|---|
| Grade A | | | |
| Grade B | | | |
| Grade C | | | |
| Total | | | |

**June**

| | Total Pay £ | Number of Employees | Average pay £ |
|---|---|---|---|
| Grade A | | | |
| Grade B | | | |
| Grade C | | | |
| Total | | | |

**July**

| | Total Pay £ | Number of Employees | Average pay £ |
|---|---|---|---|
| Grade A | | | |
| Grade B | | | |
| Grade C | | | |
| Total | | | |

**Workings for b)**

|  | Total Pay £ | Overtime Pay £ | Percentage % |
|---|---|---|---|
| **May** |  |  |  |
| **June** |  |  |  |
| **July** |  |  |  |

**Workings for c)**

|  | Sales £ | Number of employees | Sales per employee £ |
|---|---|---|---|
| **May** |  |  |  |
| **June** |  |  |  |
| **July** |  |  |  |

**2.2**

It is Asco's policy to visit their food suppliers' factories at least 3 times a year. They have given you notice that they would like to visit your factory on Monday 13<sup>th</sup> August at 1pm. One of your tasks for the week is to confirm the visit with Asco. Asco's address is Asco Ltd, Asco House, Ebony Street, Enfield, EN2 6DQ and you should reply to a Mr Michael Baron.

**Oakwood Lane**
**London,**
**N3 5RY**

PRACTICE ASSESSMENT

**2.3**

Joe Anyon has been asked to review the company's policies and procedures. He has asked you to prepare a report for him on company policies and procedures in general. You should include in your report:

- Why a company should have policies and procedures

- Which policies and procedures are required by law.

- Which policies and procedures a company should have in addition to those required by law.

- Why members of staff should adhere to the procedures.

```
REPORT

To:

From:

Date:

Subject:
```

Report (cont)

**2.4**

It is coming up to your 3 month review. Look at the job description on p168 and the person specification on p169. Relating to your own skills and experience, highlight two strengths and two weaknesses.

| STRENGTH | WEAKNESS |
|----------|----------|
| 1 | 1 |
| 2 | 2 |

**2.5**

Using your strengths and weaknesses above and your own personal career goals complete the following PDP. The first one has been completed for you.

| **Objective**. What do I want to be able to do or do better? | What will I do to achieve this? | What resources or support will I need? | Target date for completion. | With whom and when this will be reviewed. |
|---|---|---|---|---|
| 1 Gain a qualification in Accounting. | Complete my AAT level 2 Certificate in Accounting | Study time and time off for exams | September 2014 | Joe Anyon at 3 month review. |
| | | | | |
| | | | | |
| | | | | |
| | | | | |
| | | | | |

# PRACTICE ASSESSMENT

**Practice Assessment**

**for**

**AAT Level 2 Certificate**

# Work Effectively in Accounting and Finance

**SUGGESTED ANSWERS**

# Part 1

### Task 1.1

Rachel Daly is the Assistant Management Accountant. She will provide information on costs or future planning. The information she may supply will probably be any variation between expected and actual costs.

### Task 1.2

The management accounts will highlight any variances between actual and expected costs. This will ensure that costs which are rising beyond expectations can be identified at an early stage. Measures can then be taken to control the costs before they become unmanageable.

### Task 1.3

A business is required by law to have policies covering:

- Health and Safety (HASAW Act)

- Confidentiality (Data Protection Act)

- Maintaining Accounting Records (Companies Act)

- Payroll Processing (Finance Act)

- Retaining Documentation (Limitations Act)

A business will also commonly have policies on:

- Code of Conduct

- Ordering goods and services

- Making payments

- 'Green' issues.

(Choose two from each. Other answers are possible)

**1.4**

a)     Joe Anyon

b)     Remi Allen

c)     Jake Sheridan

d)     Nicola Hobbs

e)     Sales Manager (not Tyrone Thompson)

**1.5**

| | |
|---|---|
| **From:** | **s.bradley@kempfoods.com** |
| **To:** | **j.clarke@kempfoods.com** |
| **Date:** | **29th June 20XX** |
| **Subject:** | **Petty Cash Procedures** |

Hello Jess

Please find below an email which I think would be suitable to be sent to all departments to clarify the policy.

There have been a number of occasions where company policy on petty cash has not been followed. Please consider the following points

- The petty cash for each department is the responsibility of the nominated manager.

- Petty cash must not be used for personal purposes, borrowed for any purpose, used to cash personal cheques or used for any purposes outside the recognised business of Kemp Foods.

- All requests for payments from petty cash must be made to the nominated manager and they must be accompanied by a valid VAT receipt.

- The nominated manager must record all payments from petty cash on the blue voucher, stating the amount paid, a description of the goods and the reason for the payment. The receipt must be attached to the blue voucher and the blue voucher must be signed by the nominated manager.

- No single amount should be paid from petty cash in excess of £50.00

Following this policy ensures that money is available for all departments, and that small items can be paid for as efficiently and effectively as possible. If the policy is not followed there could be a shortage of money available or money could go missing from the tin. The company could have excessive expenses either from stolen money or from buying unnecessary goods.

If there is no valid voucher or receipt, the expense will not be reimbursed. Breaches of this policy may result in disciplinary action being taken.

(Remember that marks are awarded for format, layout, presentation, spelling and grammar.)

# PRACTICE ASSESSMENT

**1.6**

| | Monday<br>2nd July | Tuesday<br>3rd July | Wednesday<br>4th July | Thursday<br>5th July | Friday<br>6th July |
|---|---|---|---|---|---|
| 9.00 – 10.00 | JC1 | JC2 | JC2 | JC3 | JC2 |
| 10.00 – 11.00 | JC2 | BH2 | JC4 | JC2 | JC6 |
| 11.00 – 12.00 | TT3 | TT2 | JC4 | JC8 | JC6 |
| 12.00 – 13.00 | TT3 | TT2 | JC4 | LUNCH | LUNCH |
| 13.00 – 14.00 | LUNCH | LUNCH | LUNCH | TT1 | JC5 |
| 14.00 – 15.00 | BH2 | TT2 | JC4 | TT1 | JC5 |
| 15.00 – 16.00 | BH2 | TT2 | JC3 | BH1 | JC5 |
| 16.00 – 17.00 | BH2 | JC4 | JC3 | BH1 | JC9 |
| Possible<br>17.00 – 18.00 | BH2 | JC4 | JC3 | JC7 | TT4 |

There is room for some variation but some tasks MUST be as follows:

JC1 and TT1 are not moveable (without agreement).

JC2 must appear every day before 12pm.

JC4 must be before JC6.

JC5 cannot take place before 12pm on Friday.

JC8 cannot take place during overtime as the staff will have gone home.

**Problems identified:**

You will need to agree overtime every day.

JC3 will need an extended deadline. (JC4 will take priority over JC3 as Joe Anyon will be waiting for the work you have completed). You must agree this with Jess Clarke.

Even if you start TT4 on Friday evening it will not be completed until 1pm on Monday. (You will have the meeting with Jess and the post to complete on Monday morning as well). You must speak to Jess Clarke or Tyrone Thompson to agree a later deadline.

**1.7**

Tyrone resents staff taking time off for what he sees as non-work related matters. He doesn't see any value in learning new skills, particularly if it is not immediately evident that they will be useful.

Tyrone may make the working relationship difficult. He has to provide you with a work schedule each week so his annoyance could result in either giving you too much work, or giving you only menial tasks to do.

Not only would this make for a difficult working relationship with Tyrone, but it could also result in a reduction in efficiency and effectiveness in the office. If he were to overburden you with work there is every possibility that some jobs would not get done. If he gives you only menial tasks you would not be able to help improve the efficiency of the office.

Tyrone may also feel threatened. He has no qualifications and he may see you as a threat to his position in the office if you finish up being more qualified than him.

It may be best to start by talking to Tyrone directly. You should point out that your AAT course will be beneficial both to you and to Kemp Foods. The course will help you to learn skills which will ensure your work is both efficient and up to date. You may even learn how to do more varied work for Tyrone, leaving him free to do other tasks.

You should point out that it is company policy to allow each member of staff to carry out their Continuing Professional Development (CPD). CPD is an investment that an individual makes in him/herself. It's a way of planning individual development that links learning directly to practice. CPD can help a person keep skills up to date. It can boost confidence, strengthen professional credibility and help employees become more creative in tackling new challenges. CPD makes working life more interesting and can significantly increase job satisfaction. (It may well be wise to avoid mentioning career advancement or achieving career ambitions at the moment).

You should point out that there will be some staff members who belong to a professional body. It will be a requirement that the member carries out CPD on a regular basis. Some professional bodies even stipulate a minimum number of hours.

You should always act courteously and professionally, even if Tyrone gets annoyed or angry.

You may want then to leave the situation for a few weeks to see if his attitude towards you changes. If not you should discuss the problem with Jess. Jess is professionally at the same level as Tyrone, so she may hold more credibility to the argument.

If the situation gets no better and you feel that Tyrone is not being fair to you, you may have to resort to the grievance procedure. This must be a last resort as it will undoubtedly include a meeting with Joe Anyon and may increase Tyrone's resentment of you and your CPD. However, a solution to the problem must be found.

(Students will not be expected to give such a detailed answer, but the basic points should be covered).

# Part 2

**2.1**

**May**

|  | Total Pay £ | Number of Employees | Average pay £ |
|---|---|---|---|
| Grade A | 128581 | 83 | 1549.17 |
| Grade B | 35750 | 20 | 1787.50 |
| Grade C | 10130 | 5 | 2026.00 |
| Total | 174461 | 108 | 1615.38 |

**June**

|  | Total Pay £ | Number of Employees | Average pay £ |
|---|---|---|---|
| Grade A | 136045 | 105 | 1295.67 |
| Grade B | 32890 | 22 | 1495.00 |
| Grade C | 10166 | 6 | 1694.33 |
| Total | 179101 | 133 | 1346.62 |

**July**

|  | Total Pay £ | Number of Employees | Average pay £ |
|---|---|---|---|
| Grade A | 138298 | 101 | 1369.29 |
| Grade B | 33540 | 21 | 1597.14 |
| Grade C | 10497 | 6 | 1749.50 |
| Total | 182335 | 128 | 1424.49 |

**Workings for b)**

|       | Total Pay £ | Overtime Pay £ | Percentage % |
|-------|-------------|----------------|--------------|
| May   | 174461      | 47581          | 27.27        |
| June  | 179101      | 23361          | 13.04        |
| July  | 182335      | 32402          | 17.77        |

**Workings for c)**

|       | Sales £   | Number of employees | Sales per employee £ |
|-------|-----------|---------------------|----------------------|
| May   | 1,153,843 | 108                 | 10,683.73            |
| June  | 1,442,304 | 133                 | 10,844.39            |
| July  | 1,413,458 | 128                 | 11,042.64            |

**2.2**

**Oakwood Lane**
**London,**
**N3 5RY**

Asco Ltd
Asco House,
Ebony Street,
Enfield
EN2 6DQ

3$^{rd}$ August 2014

Dear Mr Baron,

<u>Forthcoming Visit</u>

We wish to confirm your visit with us on Monday 13$^{th}$ August at 1pm. When you arrive at reception one of our sales managers will meet you and your team members and escort you on a tour of the factory. Members of our production team will be happy to answer any questions you may have.

We look forward to your visit.

Yours sincerely

Sophie Bradley
Accounts Clerk

(Students should ensure the correct format and that there are no grammatical or spelling mistakes. It should be dated. It should begin with 'Dear Mr Baron' and end with 'Yours sincerely'. It should be short and to the point.)

**2.3**

---

## REPORT

To:     Joe Anyon, Senior Financial Accountant

From:  Sophie Bradley, Accounts Clerk

Date:  3<sup>rd</sup> August 2014

Subject:        Company Policies and Procedures.

**Why a company should have policies and procedures.**

All businesses need policies and procedures. There are processes within an organisation which are fundamental to the success of the business. These processes must be properly guided by management, performed in a consistent way, ensure the needs of the organisation are met and the correct information is collected and communicated to others. In addition, a company's policies and procedures will ensure that the organisation complies with legal requirements.

The procedures may be to ensure safety, confidentiality, maintaining quality, maintaining the correct image for the company, or simply guidance. Procedures do not have to be written, but those which are not written can lead to unacceptably different approaches, which can result in inconsistent and inefficient practices, and conflict between staff members.

**Which policies and procedures are required by law.**

Some policies and procedures are required by law (legislation).

Health & Safety is required by law. It requires employers of five or more people to have a written statement of health and safety policy. Failure to comply with Health & Safety law can result in fines or, in the most serious of cases, imprisonment for up to two years.

Businesses are required by law to keep personal details secret. While it is no requirement for a written policy on confidentiality, a company would be well advised to have one. The inadvertent release of personal details is still a criminal offence. A company should have policies such as switching off the computer screen when not in use, or not leaving personal paper files open on the desk. Only personal details are covered by legislation, but a company may well want to have further procedures in place to prevent sensitive company details falling into the hands of a competitor.

---

A business has a duty to keep accounting records. A sole trader is required by law to keep a record of income and expenditure over a period of 12 months. Limited companies must keep much more formal accounting records, following set procedures.

A business is required by law to keep full and accurate payroll records for each employee for the current and previous three tax years. Every employer must file an annual return for the payroll records (a P14 and a P35). This must be submitted by 19th May each year. A fine will be imposed if it is late. Keeping the payroll records accurate and up to date is essential for the efficiency and solvency of a business since a business is required to pay its employees, even in preference to its suppliers.

Documents must be retained for the required period set by law. How long will depend on the nature of the documents, but accounting records should in general be kept for six years from the end of the tax year to which they relate. In effect this will mean keeping records for seven years.

Some companies in certain business sectors are required by law to have further policies and procedures. The oil and chemical industry, for example, have strict regulations on avoiding pollution.

**Which policies and procedures a company should have in addition to those required by law.**

Policies and procedures are fundamental to the success of a business. Apart from those policies required by law, a company should consider further policies and procedures to maintain the company's image, to maintain quality and to ensure the right information is given to the right people at the right time.

A code of conduct should be considered. This sets out the general proper practices and responsibilities of the individuals within the organisation. Not turning up to work drunk may seem obvious, but if it's not written down the company will have little say if it actually happens.

Following a code of conduct should be a grievance procedure and a disciplinary procedure. Employers use disciplinary procedures to tell employees that their performance or conduct isn't up to the expected standard and to encourage improvement. Grievances are concerns, problems or complaints that employees raise with their employer. While a grievance procedure is not a legal requirement, a company will have less chance of winning if the employee decides to take their claim to an industrial tribunal.

Policies on ordering goods and services should be in place. If there are none, ordering items could become chaotic. If you don't know who should order the goods and when, there will either be no order at all as it will not be clear who should be ordering what, or there will be duplicate orders or over-ordering.

Policies on making payments are vital to the solvency of the company. If the company enjoys a credit facility with its supplier, paying too early will lose the benefit. In addition, if no one is sure who has paid what and when, there is a real danger that items will be paid twice.

If a company offers customers credit facilities, they should have credit control procedures. This should lay out what to do when a debt becomes overdue. Care must be taken not to upset customers who have made a genuine mistake, but at the same time customers must be made aware that they should pay on time.

Many companies will have policies on helping the environment. Recycling, saving energy and cutting down unnecessary journeys are all popular policies for companies.

**Why members of staff should adhere to the procedures.**

With some company policies it will be clear why they are in place. Health & Safety, for example, is there to protect the employee from potentially dangerous and health threatening situations. Other procedures will not be so clear.

Some policies will set out the correct format of some documents and data records. If this is not followed it could mean that the person using the document or data records will have to spend time and effort rearranging the data to fit their own needs.

Some policies will be in place simply to give a good impression to the customer.

While procedures should be reviewed from time to time, to fit the constantly changing demands of the workplace, procedures should not be ignored or changed without the proper consultations.

**2.4**

The student should assess their own skills against the job description and the person specification.

**2.5**

The student should make suitable suggestions according to their role in the scenario and also in relation to their career goals. Suitable target dates should be set.

# INDEX

# INDEX

# INDEX